# GREED

## ECONOMICS AND ETHICS IN CONFLICT

James M. Childs Jr.

**FORTRESS PRESS**
Minneapolis

*To Jenny, for her keen sense of justice and her love of community*
*To Angie, for her great generosity and her profound loyalty*
*To Becky, for her strong nurturing love and her*
*discerning sensitivity*

GREED
Economics and Ethics in Conflict

Scripture quotations from the New Revised Standard Version of the Bible are copyright © 1989 by the Division of Christian Education of the National Council of Churches of Christ in the United States of America and are used by permission.

Excerpt of "There Are Roughly Zones" from *The Poetry of Robert Frost*, edited by Edward Connery Latham. Copyright 1936 by Robert Frost, © 1964 by Lesley Frost Ballantine, © 1969 by Henry Holt and Company, reprinted by permission of Henry Holt and Company, LLC.

Interior design: Julie Odland

**Library of Congress Cataloging-in-Publication Data**
Childs, James M. (     )
    Greed : economics and ethics in conflict / James M. Childs, Jr.
        p.    cm.
    Includes bibliographical references and index.
    ISBN: 0-8006-3230-3 (alk. paper)
        1. Wealth—Moral and ethical aspects.    2. Avarice.    3. Economics—Religious aspects—Christianity.    I. Title.

HB835. C48  2000
178—dc21                                                          99-059243

Manufactured in the U.S.A.                                        AF 1-3230

04    03    02    01    00    1    2    3    4    5    6    7    8    9    10

# CONTENTS

# PREFACE

THE WITNESS OF THE CHRISTIAN ETHIC is seldom more relevant than when it addresses greed. Greed in all its manifestations has a profoundly deleterious effect on everything from the quality of personal relationships to the just distribution of goods and the future of our environment. The Christian ethic of love with its commitment to sharing and generosity, reflecting God's love and generosity, points away from the selfishness of greed toward the building of caring communities. In this book I want to draw out this contrast and make it the catalyst for shaping a thoughtful, faithful, and powerful Christian witness in economic life.

The issues dealt with here are a natural outgrowth of previous work. Concerns prompted by decades of teaching in social ethics and years of dialogue with business leaders were brought together in the 1995 publication of my book *Ethics in Business: Faith at Work*. In that book I sought to bring the Christian ethic to bear upon issues at the intersection of business and society and to encourage Christians in business to do likewise. I stand by the encouragement in that book that we can make a difference and have a vocation to try. This book reaffirms that calling and broadens the scope of concern somewhat. It also seeks to grapple with a number of distressing developments in economic life that had not fully emerged at the time of writing *Ethics in Business: Faith at Work* or had not been a part of its focus. In a sense, this grappling follows up a thread of Christian realism about human behavior and institutions that had been woven into the previous work. However, in this book as in the others I have written, realism always coexists with idealism and hope.

The topics dealt with as illustrative of greed in its various manifestations are like cases around which to develop our thoughts. Though the book deals with greed in business, disparities in health care, and the effects of economic imbalance on global hunger, for example, it is not about those phenomena per se. It is really about how these areas of economic life provide occasions to heighten our consciousness and spur our drive for better understanding and committed Christian action and advocacy.

The completion of this book has come toward the end of a wonderful sabbatical year during which I had the freedom and support to pursue this work and other projects as well. Therefore, my first expression of gratitude goes to Trinity Lutheran Seminary in Columbus, Ohio, its President, Dennis Anderson, and the Board of Directors for the generous sabbatical program we enjoy and for granting my request for this leave. Additional thanks are due my colleagues on the faculty for their support of my work and my students for the inspiration and energy they continually provide.

During the past six years I have had the pleasure of teaching a course in the MBA program of the Capital University Graduate School of Administration entitled Business and Society. This experience and the expectations of the students have helped keep me in ever-fresh dialogue with the business dimensions of economic life and the issues of ethics involved in a global economy. It has been a wonderful venue for my own growth of understanding. I am especially grateful to my friend and team-teaching colleague in that course, Professor Michael Distelhorst of the Capital University Law School faculty. Sharing with him has been enriching and challenging.

Special thanks go to Dr. Jim Nash, a colleague in the field of Christian ethics, with whom I have had the privilege of working in several projects. Jim read the manuscript prior to publication and made some helpful suggestions, which I was able to incorporate. I trust that his distinguished record in the field of ethics will be in no way diminished by his kindness in being associated with this humble work.

This is now the third book I have published with Michael West, senior editor at Fortress Press. It is high time I said publicly that working with him has been a genuine pleasure. I thank him for his encouragement, patience, and helpful suggestions all along the way.

The privilege of writing books and engaging in the research and interactivity that fuels them does not happen without enduring structures of support. I am blessed to still have my father with us in our home. He has provided friendship, love, and support throughout my life. My spouse, Linda, has made our home a place of sharing and, therefore, a source of real-life inspiration for the concerns of this book.

Among my wonderful children, the three oldest are the ones to whom this book is dedicated. I have named them with virtues that they display, which exemplify in some significant ways the ideals of the faith that drive this book. They doubtless each have many of these same traits in common, but each are special and distinct individuals and I think of each of them in special ways, even as I love them all with a special love.

# 1
# GREED:
# A CHARACTER FOR ALL SEASONS

T HE OPULENCE OF KING TUT'S TOMB and the ancient Egyptian
proverb of 2400 B.C.E., "Beware an act of avarice; it is a bad and
incurable disease," tell us that greed has some age on it. It is a
perennial human vice, a genuine character for all seasons. Certainly,
that gilded age of the pharaohs has had its counterparts at various
times and places throughout history, notably our own gilded age of
nineteenth-century American "robber barons."

M. Hirsch Goldberg's *The Complete Book of Greed: The
Strange and Amazing History of Human Excess* supplies a selective
chronicle of human avarice that demonstrates its perennial vitality as
well as displays some of its more bizarre manifestations.

Among them, the astounding tale of the head of the Southern
Pacific Railroad. Having built a $2 million mansion in New York,
he was so excessively wealthy that he could afford to indulge his
superstitious whim not to live in it. It seems a rival baron had built
one several years before and died shortly after moving in, a fate this
Southern Pacific mogul feared for himself if he were to occupy his
new home. A Nevada mine owner who bought the most expensive
property in New York and went on to spend nearly a half million
dollars decorating it certainly qualifies as another case of conspicuous opulence. Goldberg also describes lavish dinners at which the
richest of the rich could display their extravagance. At one such
party guests were given cigarettes wrapped in hundred-dollar bills.
At another dinner, given in honor of the host's dog, festivities were
capped off by the dog being presented with a $15,000 diamond
collar.[1]

Of course, the pharaohs and barons have nothing on us. For
many in this latter part of the twentieth century, a memorable dec-

laration from the movie *Wall Street,* namely, "Greed is good," has become a mantra for the American lifestyle. The last two decades have seen such phenomena as the celebration of excess on Robin Leach's popular *Lifestyles of the Rich and Famous,* soaring pay packages for CEOs, and dreams of lottery and sweepstakes windfalls. Greedy practices and fantasies continue unabated.

Greed is not all ostentation and spending or the lust for great wealth. It is also manifest in the hoarding compulsion that turns people into misers. Again, Goldberg offers some cases in point. Probably the best-known miser Goldberg cites is J. Paul Getty, whose acts of stinginess were legendary and legion. The most memorable act was Getty's decision to install a guest pay phone in his mansion for local and long-distance calls. He posted a sign that read "Public Telephone" and locked all the other phones in the house, even though at that time, 1959, it only cost eighteen cents to call from New York to London and five cents for a local call! As remarkable as this story is, it is trumped, I think, by Goldberg's brief account of a wealthy French winemaker. Having lost $75,000 in a speculative venture, he became terribly distraught, notwithstanding the fact that his estate was still worth $2 million, a princely sum in 1934. So upset was he that he went to the local store and haggled with the clerk over the price of a piece of rope. After bargaining down to the best price he could get, he took the rope home and hanged himself with it.[2]

Although saddening, these colorful examples of greed provide a sharply punctuated introduction to this discussion. They do more than simply grab our attention, however. They highlight the element of excess that is at the heart of the phenomenon we call greed. The excess is not necessarily in the amount of money or goods acquired. However frequent such correlations may appear, wealth is not always correlated with greed, and greed is not always correlated with wealth. The excess is in excessive self-concern and excessive self-aggrandizement.

There are several facets to human greed. Greed or avarice is (1) the excessive desire for goods and wealth, (2) the inordinate desire for acquiring and hoarding money, and (3) closely related to covetousness, which includes the desire for the possessions of others.[3] In each nuance of greed, the self stands at the center and the community at the periphery.

## CULTURAL SCENERY: THE CONTEXT OF GREED

While the manifestations of greed are often associated with the character and actions of individuals, greed may in fact be a by-product of the economic culture. In other words, the impulses of greed may well be a force shaping the rules of economic life, which in turn stimulate and sustain greed.

A likely illustration of this phenomenon is the patron-client model of economic order that characterized ancient Rome and the Palestine of Jesus' time. Patrons were the elite who held the bulk of power and wealth. In return for the economic support and protection their wealth and power could proffer, clients (peasants on the local level and vassals on the international level) were expected to be loyal. Although such relationships were supposed to be voluntary, and could be disrupted or broken by dissatisfaction, sociologists and anthropologists make the point that this relational structure, which channeled wealth according to power and status, was embedded in the culture.[4] Individual instances of this patron-client relationship could break down, but it seems the overall pattern still dominated.

One could well argue that the rules of economic life under feudalism permitted nobles to satisfy their greed at the expense of their peasants. One might further maintain that these rules not only permitted a certain amount of greed but, in fact, encouraged or at least tempted the nobility to greed, given the assumptions of their privilege.

Even in Martin Luther's time, after the age of feudalism had passed, a vestige of that thinking seems to have remained. While in the process of discussing the beatitude on poverty of spirit, Luther offhandedly remarked, "Having money, property, honor, power, land, and servants belongs to the secular realm; without these it could not endure. Therefore a lord or prince should not and cannot be poor, because for his office and station he must have all sorts of goods like these."[5]

Though Luther would hardly countenance greed per se, his comments suggest something akin to the cultural mind-set considered here. In fact, it should probably be noted that Luther had strong feelings about greed in economic life. A sample from his treatise "On Trade and Usury" provides a taste of his attitude.

> Among themselves the merchants have a common rule which is their chief maxim and the basis of all their sharp practices, where they say

"I may sell my goods as dear as I can." They think this is their right. Thus occasion is given for avarice, and every window and door to hell is opened. What else does it mean but this: I care nothing about my neighbor; so long as I have my profit and satisfy my greed. . . . There you see how shamelessly this maxim flies in the face not only of Christian love but also natural law.[6]

If it is likely that the rules of economic life in a given society foster the greed of a privileged class, it is just as likely that members of that class had a great deal to do with writing those rules. Thus, for example, in feudal societies one might easily aver that the rise of a class of nobility included their participation in the establishment of the rules of economic life that placed wealth in their hands and gave them the right to accumulate wealth with impunity.

In our own time, we are accustomed to the argument that capitalism promotes and tolerates greed by its emphasis upon freedom over equality. The individualism so deeply ingrained in American culture often expresses itself in the triumph of freedom for personal ambition over concern for the common good. Karl Marx's critical insight that the ruling ideas are the ideas of the ruling class suggests that the greedy who prosper from a given economic system are the same people who possess the economically based political power to craft and defend that system. (While Marx wrote against the capitalism of his day, socialist and communist systems developed in his name produced their share of people greedy for power and material advantage.) One hardly needs a quotation from Marx to generate arguments for how the privileged, if not the greedy, attempt to justify and protect their wealth and privilege, and their freedom to increase both. Simple experience will suffice.

As M. Douglas Meeks has pointed out, market logic, the logic of accumulation and exchange, becomes problematic when it pretends to be the logic governing all relationships and all patterns for the distribution of all social goods. When that happens, justice is skewed, biblical notions of stewardship are impossible, and entire classes of people who cannot fit into the system are left in the lurch.[7] It is this sort of concern that moves economist Herman Daly and theologian John Cobb to challenge economists to recognize and operate on the fact that a real human being is not *Homo economicus*. Such designation is an abstraction that sees human existence in terms of economic models rather than a multidimensional focus. It is much like seeing human reality in purely spiritual terms, purely physical terms, or purely sexual terms. This kind of singular thinking about human experience abstracts what is only one dimension of life and makes it the rule for the whole. For Daly and Cobb, the effect of casting human existence in the mold of *Homo economicus* has fostered the quest for personal gain, because it offers no competing values from other aspects of a more holistic view of life. Economic incentives are the only incentives in this outlook.[8]

Philosopher Robert Nozick's proposal for distributing the benefits of the burgeoning technologies of new genetics seems almost a reductio ad absurdum of this view. Nozick believes that a genetic "supermarket" is the only just mechanism of distribution. To be sure, the wealthy will be the chief beneficiaries of this market approach, but, then, the wealthy are needed to fund these developments whose benefits will trickle down to the middle class. "For Nozick, medicine is just another marketplace: the rules of the market, like the rules of natural selection, encourage vitality among all living members of the species."[9] This is a prime example of what Jean Bethke Ehlstain has lamented as the "commodification" of all of life, a situation in which all the values and choices of life are transmogrified into commodities exchanged in accord with market forces.[10] Not surprising, then, is a recent National Public Radio report of a growing market for women to sell their eggs. Women who are unable to conceive purchase ova for use in in vitro fertilization and subsequent implantation.

This contemporary analysis recalls a message from the ancient myth of King Midas. After Dionysus granted Midas's wish that everything he touched turn to gold, the greedy king was driven to despair when this included his wife and children. Solomon Schimmel has observed that the story of Midas shows us how dehumanizing greed can be when all things, including others and ourselves, are evaluated purely in terms of monetary worth. We lose the ability to see life around us as it truly is. "Beauty, friendship, love, and life experience are assigned an economic value. If they cannot be translated into a monetary yardstick they are considered unworthy of our attention."[11]

In words that clearly apply to this discussion, Hans Küng has recently observed the current danger ". . . of elevating the sub-system of the market economy into a *total system*, so that law, politics, culture and religion are subordinated to the economy." In this scenario,

Küng says, ethics "would be sacrificed to power and money, and be replaced by what 'gives pleasure.'"[12]

When greed is an integral part of the order of economic life and the rules of economic life become the arbiters of all relations and values in society, there is an inevitable neglect of the common good. Greed is not simply an unattractive quality. It is self-centered personal expression. In the cultural support of that self-centeredness, greed contributes to serious inequities grounded in factors other than choice or chance. This is so obvious, it's a truism.

Nevertheless, we resist taking this conclusion with utmost seriousness. Certain features of our cultural outlook, nurtured by key assumptions of our regnant economic philosophy, blind us to their own influence on our lives, much in the way certain diseases of the mind prevent us from realizing that we have them.

Thus the mildly surprising conclusion that excessive wealth, if not greed itself, is tolerated—although not necessarily admired, and sometimes regulated—in our society because of two deeply entrenched habits of our cultural mind. These habits are separate but related. The first is our tendency to prioritize freedom of the individual ahead of the equality of the many. The second, a conviction that has grown up with the success of modern capitalism, is the belief that wealth is virtually always capable of expansion.

## FREEDOM AND INDIVIDUALISM

Whether or not wealth is sought, most individuals would rather have the freedom to choose their own course in life than a more equal distribution of wealth (which might limit that freedom). Furthermore, we readily acknowledge that those who wish to amass great wealth have the freedom and moral permission to do so because our belief in the virtually unlimited ability of wealth to expand means that others also have a chance at greater wealth, if they choose to pursue it. There is a great reluctance to admit that the American dream of limitless opportunity may be flawed. When confronted by the reality of yawning gaps in the distribution of goods, we often seek other reasons for the problem than those that might force us to examine our pet convictions. As one wag put it, "if you're greedy and a fan of Adam Smith, you can try to get all the money you can in the confidence that an 'invisible hand' will always be at work to adjust the supply of wealth for the greatest good."[13] Or, again, from a recent news magazine feature: "Nowadays there are few voices raised in challenge to the pursuit of wealth. Americans don't always love the rich, but they harbor the abiding hope that anybody can become prosperous."[14]

Individual freedom is precious. People have been willing to die for it. When individual freedom turns toward individualism verging on selfishness, however, the maintenance of the common good required to sustain those precious freedoms for all citizens is endangered. Many contemporary analysts, viewing a wide range of social phenomena, believe we are in just such danger. In 1985 distinguished sociologist Robert Bellah and his colleagues published *Habits of the Heart*, a much-discussed book that provided research and analysis detailing the advance of individualism and the erosion of community in America. In the tradition of Alexis de Tocqueville, whose phrase was used for their title, Bellah and company focused their concern on public character and its moral coherence: "It would be well for us to rejoin the human race, to accept our essential poverty as a gift, and to share with those in need."[15]

Bellah's work was not without its critics. Author and theologian Michael Novak, for example, chose to emphasize de Tocqueville's observation that Americans are constantly forming associations: "Recent research confirms that the associational impulse of Americans is as strong as it was in Tocqueville's time, or even stronger."[16] It is however very questionable that forming associations can be equated with sustaining communities. The commitments we make in joining and forming associations are far more restricted in scope than the rich array of commitments entailed by the mutuality of community life. By contrast, Benjamin Barber criticized the Bellah team, not for being off the mark, but for being redundant. Social criticism uncovering the triumph of autonomy and self-realization at the expense of community constitutes what Barber called a "swollen tradition." Still, it is important to reiterate these themes of the American reality, Barber says. "Americans are good at joining, but lousy at doing things together. They make excellent entrepreneurs, but only average neighbors, and abysmal citizens. It is increasingly hard for individuals to make sense of their liberty-strewn lives."[17]

Examples of what Barber calls the triumph of autonomy continue to surface. The current debate over assisted dying provides an instructive case in point. The recent emphasis on autonomy in patient's rights, their right to take responsibility for their own treatment decisions, has been a needed corrective of the paternalistic tendencies of traditional medicine. But the surge in respect for autonomy has also resulted in controversial demands for the right to receive assistance in dying.[18] There may be good ethical reasons to entertain this possibility under limited circumstances. When the argument for assisted dying is based primarily on the right to self-determination, however, there is little regard to the impact such a policy would have on others in society. How does this affect the ethos of the medical profession? Will it take the pressure off needed efforts at better pain management and more extensive hospice care? Will the right to choose assisted dying create an atmosphere in which it is expected in the interest of cost saving? Will the personal option to choose death become an avenue for those in despair who might otherwise find help? Will the right to assisted dying weaken what resolve we have to provide insurance for long-term care? This is another example of how an ethos of individualism insinuates itself into various spheres of life. It also demonstrates the fact that regard for the individual is often a mixed blessing. Respect for autonomy is a vital ethical concern. However, autonomy can also escalate into self-centeredness that is oblivious to the fact that our personal choices often have a social dimension.

Whether we are examining the social consequences of the triumph of individual choice in the matter of dying or some other context of our lives together, Benjamin Barber's comments on *Habits of the Heart* seem durable:

> We cannot be too often reminded that individualism is both a blessing and a curse; that freedom can also appear as alienation, anomie, and loneliness; and that without a sense of others and our duties to them, the sense of self and the rights attaching to it are mocking promises of a self-sufficiency the human species will never possess.[19]

## THE HABIT OF MORE

In an interesting book, *The Hunger for More: Searching for Values in an Age of Greed*, Laurence Shames writes about the peculiar features of American history and mythology that produced what he calls the "habit of more."

> There would always be another gold rush. . . . The next generation would always ferret out opportunities that would be still more lavish

than any that had gone before. America was those opportunities. . . . You banked on the next windfall, you staked your hopes and even your self-esteem on it; and this led to the national turn of mind that might be usefully thought of as the habit of more. . . . Frontier, opportunity; more. This has been the American trinity from the very start.[20]

Shames does a good job of describing our optimistic belief in the existence of virtually boundless opportunities to satisfy the ingrained habit of "more." But his real point is that such hopes are illusory. A number of key indicators, such as a steady decline in productivity growth for a period of three decades into the eighties, suggest that our optimism is misplaced. In fact, the day of boundless opportunity ceased over a hundred years ago when the actual land frontier was eclipsed by our growth. We may not be running out of wealth, drive, savvy, and opportunities, but Shames believes there are clear indications that we are running out of "more."[21] Even the prosperity of the late nineties does not entirely mitigate concerns with the patterns Shames discusses.

Illusory or not, advocates of continuous growth economics continue to argue their case with a considerable measure of optimism, as James Eggert's helpful little primer *What Is Economics?* points out. They are convinced that no limits should be set to the possibilities of growth even from the vantage point of environmental sustainability, which they believe can be dealt with through technological innovation as required. Continuous economic growth is essential and desirable for the advance of human society. Some growth advocates even assert that continuous growth is a necessary conviction if we are to hold together a racially diverse society. Only the prospect of more for everyone can offset tensions of race and class.[22] As has just been suggested, those who challenge the pro-growth thesis often do so from an environmentalist's perspective. They argue that it is necessary to set limits to the stress we put on the finite capacities of our planet if we want to sustain life, humankind, and other kind. Economic growth must be measured and limited.

Joseph Sittler, an early advocate of Christian concern for the environment, once said to a gathering of pastors that American history might well be described as a "flight to the suburbs." He referred not simply to the proclivity of Americans to move away from people they don't want to be near but also to the American sense of limitless space and opportunity to pursue personal ambitions, heedless of the limits nature must one day impose. Much like Shames, Sittler was pointing to the undaunted belief in the unending supply of "more."

The environmental angle seems to offer an insurmountable argument for the necessity of limits, but expansionist economists challenge it nonetheless. Larry Rasmussen quotes Lawrence Summers, former chief economist of the World Bank and now U.S. Secretary of the Treasury, who has mounted just such a challenge: "There are no . . . limits to the carrying capacity of the Earth that are likely to bind at any time in the foreseeable future. . . . The idea that we should put limits on growth because of some natural limit is a profound error."[23] This kind of expansionism fits economist Kenneth Boulding's description of "cowboy economics," the belief that we can have infinite growth on a finite planet. Poking fun at his own profession, Boulding said that anyone who held this conviction was either a madman or an economist.[24]

Not all who are in business and economic life are as cavalier as the "cowboys" of economics. Many are alert, environmentally aware, and nuanced in blending their commitment to future development with global sustainability. Two recent *Harvard Business Review* articles illustrate the point. One article is by a business school professor and the other an interview with the CEO of a major chemical manufacturer. Both are keenly aware of the forces that threaten to drive our planet beyond its ability to sustain its myriad life-forms. Both are clear about the impact of industry on the environment and about the necessity for business and industry to reconsider its practices in view of that impact. Both are clear that business has a key role to play in reversing environmental degradation through the development of new technologies and the institution of environmentally friendly policies and marketing. And both agree that practices and the development of technology for successfully coping with the limits of the environment opens up great opportunities for (unlimited?) growth in business.[25] The environmental sensitivities business leaders must face are understandable. Their need to look at matters in terms of long-term financial viability is a necessity. Nevertheless, if technology and expansionist economics really have brought us to the brink of our limits, is the way we got into the problem really the way out of it?

The issues of environmental ethics will be revisited later in this book. For now, it is sufficient to note that ecology is a particularly good lens for sharper visual acuity when viewing the problem of humanity's tragic defiance of its own finitude. Theologically speaking, this defiance of our ontic *limits* gives rise to the perduring *limitations* of our sinfulness. Sin is rooted in our alienation from God. It is alienation expressed in a denial of our finitude that elevates the independent self above its dependent relationship to God. This is the meaning of the Fall story.

But the serpent said, "You will not die; for God knows that when you eat of it your eyes will be opened, and you will be like God" (Genesis 3:4-5).

## A MORAL ALTERNATIVE

In contrast to the predilections of contemporary American culture, biblical and theological traditions, which inform the Christian ethic and worldview, operate with a realistic recognition of the limits of finitude and the limitations of sin. In its concern for the common good, Christian ethics brings this realism into constant dialogue with its own idealism as it seeks to shape a moral alternative to those elements of the prevailing ethos that foster greed. Voices of the Christian tradition provide the Christian community with insight and direction for its witness on behalf of those hurt most by manifestations of greed in economic life.

The prophet Isaiah pronounces a woe against those who oppress the poor by their greed, those "who join house to house, who add field to field, until there is room for no one [but them]" (Isaiah 5:8ff.). And he confronts those "who write oppressive statutes, to turn aside the needy from justice and to rob the poor of my people of their right, that widows may be your spoil, and that you may make the orphans your prey!" (10:1-2).

When Jesus inaugurates his public ministry in Luke 4 by quoting Isaiah 61:1-2 with its "good news for the poor," he echoes, along with Isaiah, the Jubilee tradition of Leviticus 25:8-10, which commands that debts be forgiven and that scattered and dispossessed families be reunited on their lands. By identifying his own person and work with that ancient concern for economic justice, Jesus lets us know that the reign of God will not brook the inequities created by greed and oppression.

Other examples of the dangers of wealth and the virtues of sharing found throughout the New Testament provide an important backdrop to this discussion. Jesus challenges the rich young man to see how his possessions stand between him and devotion to God (Matthew 19:16-30). "You cannot serve God and wealth" (Matthew 6:24). In the day of judgment compassion for those in material need will be seen as direct love of the Son (Matthew 25:34-36). Such compassion for widows in their need was a regular feature of the diaconal ministry of the Jerusalem church (Acts 6:1-6). To see one's neighbor in need and fail to help when one has the wherewithal to do so is simply inconsistent with Christian love (1 John 3:17). 1 Timothy 6:17-19 warns those who are rich not to be "haughty" or to trust in riches but rather to accumulate the wealth of good works, generosity, and readiness to share.[26]

In the next chapter we will look in greater detail at some of the biblical material critical to this discussion. In chapters 3, 4, and 5, we will look at the manifestations of greed and its progeny in the contexts of business, health care, and the global economic order, as refracted through the lens of hunger. Chapter 6 moves us toward the vision of a "sharing society," while in chapter 7 we return to the venue of business to consider stakeholder capitalism as a case study in sharing. Chapter 8 explores the sort of virtues conducive to community, those that can help offset the corrosive effects of that subtle form of greed called "consumerism." Finally, chapter 9 attempts to distill what all this means for the calling of Christian people.

In all that follows, I hope to challenge, in its personal and cultural manifestations, the self-centered refusal to recognize limits and thereby give free reign to ambition at the expense of the general well-being. My hope is that the Christian agenda for the good of all neighbors will lead you, the reader, to see that greater equality in sharing the goods of this world will in the final analysis mean greater real freedom for everyone. In this premise there is an echo of L. T. Hobhouse's classic work, *Liberalism*, in which he argued over and over again that freedom requires restraint on behalf of others because full freedom rests on equality and mutual restraint is the foundation of equality.[27] Finally, I hope to provide concrete examples and proposals of solutions that resonate with the Christian vision and sensibilities. I can honestly say that I am neither targeting nor advocating any particular economic system or political perspective. I hold democracy as the only just political alternative and the United States market economy as the most successful economic system to date. Nevertheless, even the best and the most successful systems are subject not only to the contingencies of life but, more profoundly, to the influences of character and ethos from those who work them. These—character and ethos—are my primary zone of concern.

The questions at the end of each chapter are meant to meaningfully engage you, the reader, in this discussion. That there are questions points to the fact that it is a difficult and complex discussion. There is both benefit and necessity in people of faith coming together to deliberate on such matters. What we are called to be as the people of God can be stated with considerable clarity. How we implement that in our choices and our plans, as well as how our Christian vision speaks to issues of economic life and related public policy, is not always as clear.

## QUESTIONS FOR DISCUSSION

1. What examples can you give—obvious and not so obvious—of greedy behavior on the part of both individuals and organizations?
2. What cultural influences tend to foster greed?
3. In what ways can Christianity provide a countercultural alternative for the sort of self-centered materialism associated with greed?
4. Are there bad habits or areas of neglect in the life and work of the church that unwittingly support avarice?

# 2
# FROM PARABLE TO PARADIGM

GREED IS NOT MERELY A MATTER OF INDIVIDUAL VICE. Certain features of a corporate ethos that encourages greed are woven into the fabric of economic life. The cultural impulse to value individual freedom more than the needs of the whole community is one. This, combined with a belief in the virtually limitless potential of economic growth, has allowed greed to flourish, even if all do not desire great wealth or admire those who do. Moreover, the power wealth creates, including the relative freedom from constraints of community needs, allows the affluent to influence the rules of economic life in ways that perpetuate that power and freedom. The result: too many instances in which concern for community well-being is frustrated by the ambitions of those with wealth and power. In theory, concern for individual freedom and belief in ever expanding economic opportunities should not necessarily create such imbalances, but in practice it does. This state of affairs raises some key questions.

If we really do operate on the premise that the potential for wealth to expand is, for all practical purposes, unlimited, is this a course of action we can realistically sustain? Economists disagree. Ecologists reject it, citing limits in the carrying capacity of the earth and threats to the integrity of environmental systems. Human aspirations often embrace it. Bitter experience often doubts it.

Does being realistic about the limits of economic growth not mean that the freedom of each individual to have a fair share of prosperity is a myth and equal opportunity an empty claim? Even if the limits of potential economic expansion have yet to be seen, does allowing unbridled freedom for individual gain, as well as increased prosperity for the already affluent, frustrate the opportunity of all to participate in that economic growth? To what extent must individual freedom be constrained by a responsibility to the needs of the many? If current laws and tax revenues collected and assigned to certain human services already set certain limits on individual freedom, is there need for even more constraint? Finally, is there an alternate view of socioeconomic reality apart from the one these questions challenge?

In addressing these questions, it is important to note that a new set of facts or a new set of policy options is not the paramount interest here. Rather, it is to look into the spirit of economic life by examining the soul of our culture. As noted in chapter 1, the Bible addresses socioeconomic reality and its concern for economic justice. In fact, it may well offer an alternate view of reality than that embodied in the prevailing outlook of our culture. Now it is time to take a closer look. We'll start with a parable, letting it lead us through some important themes until we reach what could be called a paradigm.

## THE RICH MAN AND LAZARUS—LUKE 16:19-31

There was a rich man who was dressed in purple and fine linen and who feasted sumptuously every day. At his gate lay a beggar named Lazarus, covered with sores, who longed to satisfy his hunger with scraps from the rich man's table. The beggar died and was carried away by the angels to be with Abraham. The rich man also died and was buried.

From Hades, the rich man looked up and saw Abraham far away with Lazarus by his side. He called out, "Father Abraham, have mercy on me. Send Lazarus to dip the tip of his finger in water and cool my tongue, for I am tormented in this flame."

But Abraham said, "Child, remember that during your lifetime you received good things, and Lazarus in like manner evil things; but now he is comforted here, and you are in agony. Besides all this, between you and us a great chasm has been fixed, so that those who might want to pass from here to you cannot do so, and no one can cross from there to us."

The rich man said, "Then, father, I beg you to send him to my father's house—for I have five brothers—that he may warn them, so that they will not also come into this place of torment."

Abraham replied, "They have Moses and the prophets; they should listen to them."

"No, father Abraham, if someone goes to them from the dead, they will repent."

Abraham answered, "If they do not listen to Moses and the prophets, neither will they be convinced even if someone rises from the dead."

I have vivid recollections of a sermon on this parable, which I heard as a young teen. The pastor took great pains to provide intense commentary on the torments of hell being experienced by the rich man. So hideous was the endless trial by fire that for Lazarus to merely dip his finger in water and touch his feverish tongue would be glorious refreshment. The message from the pastor was that the torments of hell were very real and the just desserts of those who are unrepentant, faithless, and greedy.

Equally clear is my memory of my reaction. I didn't believe him. The pastor's reflections didn't square with the understanding I had gotten, ironically, from a previous sermon by this same pastor. It seemed to me that the message of God's grace in Christ was not that God would simply condemn sinners to unremitting agony. Rather, God would make it right somehow. Surely God is not "soft" on greed, but it seemed that this was a story in need of further explanation.

As it turns out, my untutored intuition was not too far off the mark. When considering the parable more carefully, and in conjunction with other, similar parables, it becomes clear that the principle focus is on God's intention and promise to "make things right."

The story of Lazarus and the rich man is one of a number of parables that scholars often refer to as "reversal parables." These parables carry the message that in the fullness of God's coming reign, revealed and inaugurated by Jesus, the poor and the victims of injustice will find the wholeness and joy, the equality and fairness they did not know in their lifetimes. The emphasis is on the justice that will characterize God's future dominion.[1] One cannot help but hear in this story echoes of Luke 13:30: "Indeed, some are last who will be first, and some are first who will be last," a statement by Jesus also recorded in Matthew (19:30) and Mark (10:31). The scales of God's justice, born of God's love for all of creation, will be balanced.

This parable had its counterpart in the folklore of both Egyptian and Jewish traditions. In those traditions the central point was one of morality. Those who have been good and suffered will be rewarded in the life beyond; those who have done evil in this life will suffer in the next. Most interpreters note that in this parable of Jesus, this moral point is strikingly omitted, however. Nothing is said of the moral character of either the rich man or Lazarus. The disparities and inequities between rich and poor are at the center of the stage, vividly depicted by the way in which the unspeakable squalor of Lazarus is placed at the very gate of one who lives in opulence. Then, in equally stark contrast, the magnitude of God's setting things right is expressed in the heavenly bliss of Lazarus and the unspeakable suffering of the rich man in Hades.[2] This is not a story of reward and punishment based on individual moral achievement. Here as elsewhere in Luke's Gospel, the expectation of God's dominion in the fullness of time is for reversal, not revenge.[3]

The parable holds up a mirror in which to see the face of individual greed and how it finds systemic expression in the enormous disparities in quality of life across the vast global community. In a way, the parable is much like one of those makeup mirrors that magnify: we see in far greater distressing detail than we would care to.

To bring the parable closer to home, to transplant it from its first-century soil into contemporary ground, one need only reflect on commonplace experiences with the reality of poverty and desperation. Three particular moments in my life stand out.

Having flown for many sleepless hours, I arrived in Madras on my first visit to India more than ten years ago. Since I had eight hours before my flight to Bangalore, I decided to take a cab to a nearby hotel where I could book a day room and get some sleep. No sooner had I gotten into the taxi than a young Indian girl holding a tiny baby, who was covered with sores, ran up and thrust the infant through the window of the car. Holding her tiny baby in front of my face was her way of pleading for money. A very effective way, I might add. Shaken by my close encounter with that poor little baby, I arrived at my hotel, a lovely, serene spot with palm tree–lined courtyards and all the amenities of a fine hotel one might find almost anywhere in the world. This would be the first of many such experiences with dramatic contrast during my stay in that country.

More recently, on a trip to Tanzania, I had occasion to live on a college campus located in a small village. Some of my duties as a visiting scholar were to read student reports on field experiences. In them I learned firsthand of the problems of disease, abuse, homelessness, and poverty that plagued so many of the Tanzanian people.

Such accounts were easy to believe, given what I saw of the living conditions in the adjacent village and elsewhere throughout the country. Toward the end of my stay, I took an American student to dinner at a hotel in the city of Arusha. This particular hotel catered to tourists who were going on safari or those who were there to mountain climb. As we reflected on the things we had seen and learned during our stay, a group of well-fed tourists were toasting themselves for their great stamina and brave endurance on their climbing expedition. Within the confines of the scene, I could smile and accept their celebration for what it was, a fleeting moment of exhilaration and camaraderie. Within the larger context of the overwhelming poverty in that country, however, the group's self-congratulatory feting of a recreational triumph stood in glaring contrast to the heroic stamina and endurance of the average Tanzanian village woman struggling to make it through each day.

One doesn't have to visit another land to experience these types of contrasts, though. While recently in a major city in the United States, I was stunned by the large numbers of homeless people occupying corners throughout the downtown business and shopping districts. In contrast to the evident misery of the homeless and their seeming lack of hopeful prospects were the thousands of shoppers crowding the streets. It was the beginning of the commercial Christmas season and all the fine stores were decked out in Christmas glitter, piping familiar Christmas tunes into the well-heeled streets. Once again, I felt trapped in the pincers of a disturbing contrast.

Most have had such experiences, to be sure. And, most feel genuinely troubled by these sorts of encounters. It is these troubled feelings I wish to examine. They may well be a key to perceiving the message of the parable.

Combined with the feelings of sadness, dismay, pity, even anger at seeing people trapped in their suffering, we who witness such dire need often experience feelings of guilt. Guilt for our material comforts while others are suffering such hardships. Or worse, guilt that we've done nothing to help or alleviate others' pain. Even if we have given to charity or volunteered for charitable causes, we are often overtaken by a deep sense of frustration. It is not just that the task seems so immense and our efforts so small; it is also the strong underlying suspicion that things are so out of whack in the world that there is no way to put them right. Some may even wonder whether our best-intended efforts are producing harm rather than help. After all, one need only review the endless debates over welfare reform in the United States to see how cogent proposals and counterproposals can be argued with equal conviction, leaving many in a quandary as to what really is the best way to help the poor.

The sense that things are desperately out of whack in today's world has its counterpart in the cultural milieu in which the parable of the rich man and Lazarus is set. Examining that setting should tell us something about the biblical perspective on economic life in relation to community and shed further light on why this parable is a parable of "reversal."

## THE "LIMITED GOOD SOCIETY"

In contrast to the vision of economic reality in our own society, the culture of Luke's world was one marked by scarcity. This was a village society in which all of the resources were believed to be in short supply. In the patron-client system, wealthy patrons held the power and the possessions. Given this kind of entrenched inequality, there was little, if anything, peasants could do to increase their share of the good. There was no first-century version of the American dream (or myth) and no Palestinian Horatio Alger sagas to inspire the ambitious. Distribution of the good in what Halvor Moxnes has called a "limited good society" was out of whack.[4]

A key indicator of that state of affairs was the heavy burden of debt borne by so many of the peasants. This debt was a sure sign of their inescapable dependency upon those over them in the power structure. The parable of the nobleman in Luke 19:12-27 is a particularly good example of how villagers viewed the landlords, who kept them in servitude through indebtedness, as greedy and harsh. (This parable includes the narrative about use of talents. Our customary focus on this part of the story tends to overshadow the description of how hated and harsh was the nobleman and how cruel was his revenge on those who let him down or sought to shed his rule.) Peasants' indebtedness and inability to meet their obligations were signs that the social balance was upset.[5]

The key to morally acceptable economic life is not to be found in possessing or not possessing wealth, however. It is in whether or not one shares. This is the paradigm to which we are led. Sharing is the heart and core of economic life and community.

In a "limited good society" the amount of power, wealth, and other resources are held to be visibly finite. Therefore, how that limited good is distributed becomes a matter of critical moral importance (a matter of justice) far more urgent than in a society that believes in the possibility of virtually limitless economic growth. In a limited good society, if one has a great deal more, others will be consigned to having less. There is no sense of an expandable economy in which the "have-nots" can close the gap with the "haves." There are certainly moral judgments in the New Testament about how one gains wealth. The critique of the ill-gotten gains of tax collectors immediately comes to mind. However, assuming that wealth has come through honest work and good fortune, the key issue for a moral economy in the peasant world is how that wealth is used, specifically, whether or not it is shared. The rich fool of Luke 12:16-21 had a good harvest. There was nothing wrong with his attaining prosperity; he came by it honestly and by good fortune. The moral failure was not inviting others to share in his celebration and his wealth. Instead, he "guarded his wealth avariciously." Moreover, by building more barns to store his surplus, he also made sure that, if bad years were to come, villagers would have to buy from him and be dependent on him. From the vantage point of the common people, the rich fool was not only being selfish in his time of prosperity, he was also "laying up treasures for himself" into the foreseeable future.[6]

Centuries later, Luther offers a similar analysis of some of the greedy merchants of his time:

> Again, there are some who sell their goods at a higher price than they command in the common market, or than is customary in the trade; they raise the price of their wares for no other reason than because they know that there is no more of that commodity in the country. . . . That is the rogue's eye of greed, which sees only the neighbor's need; not to relieve it but to make the most of it and get rich at his expense.[7]

The inherent inequalities of the patron-client system in a society of limited good are exacerbated when the rich do not contribute to the common good. Failure to share means that some people's basic needs will not be met, needs such as food and clothing. The imperative to share is grounded, then, in a communal obligation to meet those needs. Acts 2:44-45 and 4:34-35 describe the Christian community of the apostles in which all goods were held in common and distributed to meet the needs of all. Seemingly, this is the ideal behind Luke's imperative.[8] As Walter Pilgrim has argued, the Christian community of Acts was not practicing communism, as is sometimes thought. The goods they sold and distributed to the needy were done as need arose and voluntarily. They were not required to do so as would be the case in communism. Furthermore, not all goods were sold and not all property ownership was relinquished. Simply put, theirs was a voluntary ethic of sharing that was responsive to the needs of the community. Rather than the inauguration of an economic philosophy, this was ongoing concern for community solidarity in the meeting of basic needs.[9]

Speaking of Luke's concerns in terms of familiar notions about justice, it seems legitimate to infer from Luke and Acts a plea for what would be called *equalitarian justice,* that is, justice at the level of basic life needs. Western thought about justice has usually taken its clue from Aristotle's ancient dictum that justice is done when each receives his or her "due." This was a "formal" principle. "Material" principles were needed to explain how to determine what each person is "due" in a given situation.

One material principle, for example, is that each is to be rewarded according to his or her merit. This works well when determining what grade a student receives on an exam, or which worker should get a promotion. In those cases, unequal performances merit unequal rewards. Generally, these inequalities are deemed fair. Another material principle distributes the good according to each person's ability to pay for it. Once again, many human transactions justify that there are inequalities in ability to pay for something, and that some having more than others is not necessarily unfair. After all, some people choose to have less money. Others have an innate inability to do the things required to accumulate wealth. Many may regard this as unfortunate in some cases, but not necessarily unjust. But, when people are unable to participate in opportunities to make money because they are denied fair access to those opportunities or are so deprived of education and the necessities of life that they can't compete, another material principle of justice is invoked: "to each according to their needs."

Distribution according to need is based on the premise that all people deserve to have their basic needs met, simply by virtue of their being human beings. This material principle is equalitarian: universal human need is the only basis. The implication is that a just society will make certain that these needs are met for all of its members. Those who are able to meet their own needs, and those who have a surplus, are expected to assist those who are not. Though Luke had no notion of a welfare state, he certainly voiced the same consideration as that in the material principle of need.

Jesus' indictment of the Pharisees, called "lovers of money" in Luke 16:14-15, accuses them of greed for wealth and greed for honor. In a society that understands both wealth and honor to be in limited supply, this trait of the Pharisees constitutes a rejection of community solidarity. They are willing to share neither wealth nor prestige in a measure appropriate to the equalitarian justice implicit in Luke's ethos.[10] For this reason, the Pharisees, who were champions of ritual purity, were themselves adjudged "impure" because their greed fragmented the very bonds of community that purity laws were supposed to serve.[11] As lovers of money, they are guilty of the sin of idolatry. They fail to gives alms and hospitality. Like the rich man with Lazarus, they fail to share.

Luke's portrait is not of individual sins of the Pharisees, however. It presents them as anti-types to Jesus and his followers, as stereotypes of the type of selfishness and avarice that destroys the values of sharing and community. This and their love of honor and power are what condemn them, not their wealth.[12]

Certainly, contemporary economic order is a far cry from the patron-client economy of Luke's village setting. Neither a well-developed sense of freedom nor a cogent concept of growth was present as a dissipating influence on the concern for greed. Moreover, that culture's prevailing conviction that all goods were in limited supply made issues of greed and hunger for power and honor more pronounced than they are today. Nevertheless, there is still at least one parallel to consider.

As discussed earlier, when the rules of economic life favor the fortunes of an elite class, the power wealth confers likely has been used to write and perpetuate those rules. That is evident in the way the patron-client economic system operated. It is also evident in the desire of the Pharisees to seek status, power, and money at the expense of equalitarian values of community and provision for the basic needs of all. Consider the following statement from a recent study.

In general, people go hungry because they are poor and powerless. To achieve food security, they need both income and power. In the United States, poor people have suffered disproportionate losses in recent debates over the federal budget. Low-income people tend not to vote, and the organizations that represent them are much weaker than many other interests.[13]

Greedy people hoard both wealth and power; the two go together. In contemporary circumstances, as in Luke's world, things are seriously out of whack and in need of reversal. Moreover, those seeking to hoard both power and wealth find it easy to exploit the latitude our culture of personal freedom provides. In a culture where the common good is the higher priority, as in the Palestine of the New Testament, wealth uses power to seek its own ends anyway. In both cases, the poor are not likely to experience much in the way of freedom or equality, let alone any sense of unlimited opportunities. The limitation of sin, that state of self-centeredness, exemplified by greed, restricts our capacity to be concerned about the well-being of others.

These reflections on Scripture lead, then, to questioning the extent to which we should place limits on our individual freedom and the way in which the self-centeredness of our sinful nature places limitations on our capacity to do so. A shift from sociological reflection on the biblical world to a look at biblical anthropology can amplify that discussion.

## FROM SOCIOLOGY TO ANTHROPOLOGY

The key theological term for biblical anthropology is *image of God*. Genesis 1:26 reads, "Then God said, 'Let us make humankind, in our own image, according to our likeness; and let them have dominion.'" In this verse and the one that follows (". . . in the image of God he created them; male and female he created them.") some of the main features of biblical anthropology are nascent in the narrative, which forms the immediate context of the passage, and in the metaphorical force of the Hebrew words for *image* and *likeness*.

First of all, when God says, "Let us make humankind in our image," a decided break in the narrative pattern signals something new is happening. In previous verses, God calls upon the waters and the earth to bring forth all other living things. The elements are participants in that creation. But the creation of humankind is unmediated. The plants, for example, have an indirect relationship to God, mediated through the ground. The animals also have their immediate relationship to the soil. Nothing stands between God and humankind. The creation of humanity is unique in this respect and sets humankind apart for a special place in the created order.[14]

The immediacy of the relationship between God and humanity is nowhere more profoundly expressed than in the idea of covenant, which is sustained throughout the Bible. In God's covenant, humanity is embraced and addressed by the promises of a loving God. Both the people of ancient Israel and of the new Israel experience God in intensely personal terms. Created for this relationship, a personal relationship with God constitutes the very being of humankind. When that relationship is intact, humanity's existence is authentic. "[Humanity] has a share in the personhood of God; and, as being capable of self-awareness and of self-determination, he [sic] is open to the divine address and capable of responsible conduct."[15]

The freedom and responsibility at the core of personhood in relation to God is the basis of our call to exercise "dominion" over the earth (Genesis 1:28). But, it is a call under the imperative to love and care for the earth as its creator does, not to exploit it or do with it as we wish.[16] Living under this divine imperative, inherent in our creation, underscores another feature of humanity's creation in the image of God. Our sovereignty, if that term is at all meaningful, is representational. The clue is in the meaning of the Hebrew word for "image," *tselem*. *Tselem* is literally an image in the sense of a carved or hewn copy of something else. Just as powerful kings in the ancient world placed their *tselem* (statues of themselves) to represent their sovereignty in territories where they were not present, so we, as God's *tselem*, merely represent God in the care of the creation.[17]

The impact of the "image" metaphor should, then, be clear. Though created for special relationship with God and, as such, unique among creatures, humankind is still "image" of God, not God. Our very being is dependent being. The temptation proffered by the serpent in the Garden of Eden is for Adam and Eve to step beyond the limits of dependent being, to "be like God" (Genesis 3:5). Their decision to go beyond their limits and turn their backs on God is the essence of the fall, which inaugurates the limitation of human sin. One might simply add that recent failure to respect the limits of the environment serves as a contemporary parable for the message of the fall. Called to care for the earth, human beings have stepped outside divine vocation and exploited it. By not respecting limits, we manifest our limitation.

Robert Frost's poem, "There Are Roughly Zones," captures the poignancy of the human condition in reflecting upon a small event in humanity's ambiguous relation to the nature entrusted to it. Men sit indoors on a bitter cold night wondering whether the peach tree they admittedly brought too far north will survive the cold.

> It is very far north, we admit, to have brought the peach.
> What comes over a man, is it soul or mind—
> That to no limits and bounds he can stay confined?
>
> . . .
>
> The tree has no leaves and may never have them again.
> We must wait till some months hence in the spring to know.
> But if it is destined never again to grow,
> It can blame this limitless trait in the hearts of men.[18]

The idea of *limit* is not only a quantitative term, as in the limits of our resources or the finite character of our existence. The idea of *limit* is community. We are limited by neighbors' needs, and we are limited by our responsibility for those needs in our community of co-humanity. This dimension of the notion of limits dovetails with the understanding of human freedom that is entailed in reflecting further on creation in the divine image. As people whose very being is constituted by relationship with God and dependent upon it, the freedom inherent in our personhood must be understood accordingly. We are at the core of our existence "relational," created for community with God and each other. In reflecting on the creation of humanity in Genesis 1, Dietrich Bonhoeffer observed that freedom is not something human beings possess as a quality. It is something that exists only in relationship to the other, God and our neighbors. "In truth, freedom is a relationship between two persons. Being free means 'being free for the other,' . . . Only in relationship with the other am I free."[19]

In the biblical understanding of anthropology, human freedom and authentic personhood is sustained, not in an individualistic notion of freedom from the needs and concerns of community, but in recognizing and living out the community with God and neighbor that is constitutive of our being created in the image of God.

Indeed, when we follow the anthropological strand of the image-of-God doctrine into the New Testament, we find this sense of ineluctable connectedness to the neighbor strengthened by the example of Christ's self-limiting love (Philippians 2:4ff.). Jesus is our prototype in a twofold sense: he is the revelation of God in whose image we shall be perfected in the resurrection (1 Corinthians 15, especially vv. 44-49), and he is the revelation of what true authentic humanity is all about. Christ reveals the future of our humanity, which defines the truth and hope of our existence in the present. We are what we shall be. We are raised and exalted with Christ in baptism. This baptism in Christ to a new creation is a renewal after the image of God (Colossians 3:9-11 and Ephesians 2:22-24). What is thus inaugurated is brought to completion in the fullness of God's future (2 Corinthians 3:18).[20]

The self-limiting, self-emptying love of the Christ described in Philippians 2 is the standard of neighbor love. This love is an integral part of what it means to exist in the authentic humanity of our destiny as people created and redeemed in the image of God. This link between our existence in the image of God and the neighbor love of Christ, our prototype, means that *image of God* includes our intimate relationship of mutual love in communion and union with God as well as love of our neighbor. The great theologian Karl Barth has an interesting slant on this point. He underlines the fact that God created us in the divine image as male and female. He considers this primordial relationship of community between woman and man to be an analog for the larger truth that we are created for loving community with our neighbors.[21]

As Jesus is united in love with the Father and the Spirit in the community of the Trinity, and with us in our humanity, so we are created in the image of God for community both with God and one another.

As was suggested at the end of the first chapter, the Bible is filled with instances in which sharing and mutual concern is lifted up as a norm of Christian life. One more example can round out this discussion. In the Epistle of James is this admonition in the context of the famous assertion that faith without works is dead: "If a brother or sister is naked and lacks daily food, and one of you says to them, 'Go in peace; keep warm and eat your fill,' and yet you do not supply their bodily needs, what is the good of that?" (James 2:15-16). Failure to share with sisters and brothers in need stands condemned within the community of faith. Moreover, that censure extends beyond the congregation to those rich who have exploited people rather than dealing justly and generously with them (James 5:1-6).

In God's dealings with us, the reality of need is the necessity of love. In our dealings with our neighbors, the same formula applies.[22] The ethical vocation of God's people is the reenactment of God's acts of love and justice.[23]

## A PEOPLE OF ANTICIPATION

This chapter has examined some key features of the biblical witness related to our concerns with greed, both in its individual expressions and its socially embedded forms. Now, in conclusion, I want to raise an imperative implicit in the parable of Lazarus and the rich man. As noted, the parable is expressive of a larger Lukan theme of eschatological reversal. The tragic imbalances of wealth in the world, so dramatically illustrated by the contrast between the rich man and Lazarus, and the suffering that ensues, so poignantly depicted in the abject misery of Lazarus, will be set right in the fullness of God's coming reign. We who have been privileged by grace in faith to see the truth of this promise revealed in Christ are, as his people, his continuing presence on earth, called to anticipate this promise in our own sharing and in our own striving for economic justice. If "the reality of need is the necessity of love" for God and for us, it is certainly consistent with a prominent theme in Luke's Gospel, hinted at in the parable of the rich man and Lazarus: the people of God are to be in solidarity with those in need.[24] This is the paradigm to which the parable has led us: economic life is to be founded on a community of sharing.

This is all well and good, and undoubtedly true, but what does it mean concretely for our witness as a Christian people? What do we have to say at this intersection of God's word and our world, and how do we go about saying it? These are the questions to be addressed in the chapters that follow as we continue the dialogue between the Christian faith and the worldly realities of economic life. Sharing is an outlook, a disposition of love, an orientation of character faithfully trying to find its way through what is often a maze of confusing circumstances.

# QUESTIONS FOR DISCUSSION

1. What other stories or passages from the Bible belong in this discussion of greed and sharing?

2. Is it true that we are more concerned with individual freedoms and personal goals than we are with the welfare of all in our communities? What experiences have you had that support that opinion? What experiences have you had that give an opposite picture?

3. Are there ways in which we can reinforce a sense of community responsibility and concern for the needs of others in our congregational life and activities?

4. What are the avenues we have for sharing? Is the creation of wealth through good business and hard work a form of sharing because it contributes jobs, tax revenues, and the opportunity for subsidiary enterprises?

# 3
# THE BUSINESS OF BUSINESS IS AVARICE?

In the tenth anniversary issue of *Business Ethics* magazine, editor Marjorie Kelly led off with the following remarks:

> I found in my files the other day a dog-eared set of overheads, "Ten Trends Toward Socially Responsible Business"—the verbal bones of what for years was my standard speech. It was a can-do, chin-up kind of talk about environmentalism, family-friendly policies, employee ownership, codes of conduct, cause-related marketing, participatory management, and the rest. It's not a speech I give anymore.[1]

She goes on to delineate the source of her disenchantment in the signs of an intransigent feudalism displayed in corporate practices and attitudes that continue to reward wealthy stockholders at the expense of one of the principal stakeholders, the employees.

Ms. Kelly reflects the malaise of a good number of Americans. After a surge of interest in more ethical business following the greed and scandals of the eighties, corporate America appears to many to have returned to business as usual. The nineties became the decade of downsizing and excessive pay packages for top management. For employees, this has meant heavier workloads and lower wages while corporate profits continue to grow. The hoarding of wealth and power in economic life seems to be as virulent as ever.

There has certainly been considerable discussion of both downsizing and executive compensation issues and their impact on the lives of Americans.[2] Nevertheless, no discussion of the type presented here can ignore this phenomenon of contemporary economic life.

## THE DOWNSIDE OF DOWNSIZING: GREED OR NEED?

March 3, 1996, marked the beginning of a seven-part series in the *New York Times* entitled "The Downsizing of America." The series provided a distressing damage report, documenting the painful effects of massive layoffs due to what is euphemistically referred to as "corporate restructuring." For example, a fifty-one-year-old loan officer who now works at a roadside tourist center for a fourth of what he once made lost not only his job but his wife and the esteem of his children along with it. Individual tragedies like this particular case put a human face on the statistics, although the statistics are certainly startling enough. In the downsizing spree of the nineties, AT&T led the way by cutting 123,000 jobs, Sears came in second with a 50,000-job reduction, Delta Airlines dropped 18,800 employees, and Eastman Kodak eliminated 16,800 jobs.[3]

As middle-class, white-collar workers join the ranks of the working class and the poor in a state of chronic economic insecurity, attitudinal changes become more and more evident. People overtaken by weariness and frustration begin to withdraw from community service. It is more and more difficult to find volunteers for charity drives, or someone to lead a scout troop or coach a Little League team. What's more, the losses of downsizing tend to foster intolerance and prejudice: people who are hurt and angry often search for scapegoats. As the *Times* article put it, "Job apprehension has intruded everywhere, diluting self-worth, splintering families, fragmenting communities, altering the chemistry of workplaces, roiling political agendas and rubbing salt on the very soul of the community."[4] If career building in business has usually been thought of in terms of individual ambition, setbacks and community consequences caused by downsizing display the reality of our inescapable interconnectedness. Individualism may be our cultural credo, but the organic relatedness of life in community is our true state of affairs.

Beyond the harm done to individuals and communities, the downsizing phenomenon has also revealed how economic life has, to use the phrase again, gotten out of whack. Another 1996 article reported that workers who lose their jobs in restructuring—200,000 during that year alone—earn about 10 percent less in their next job, should they be fortunate enough to find one. In fact, the largest-growing segment of the workforce is temporary employment, which earns about 35 percent less than the average full-time worker.[5] While corporate profits have risen in the 15-percent range in recent years, the salary of the average worker has risen by less than 3 percent and others in the workforce, as just noted, have taken losses.[6]

As the downsizing splurge reached its height in 1996, columnist Russell Baker attacked those high-salaried elites who defend downsizing and preach market values to its victims. He concluded his editorial assault with this quote: "To be thrown out of work after 20 years with the same firm, as if we were of no more value than a piece of worn-out machinery, is, indeed, to feel like a piece of junk."[7]

Clearly, an emotionally charged issue like downsizing is easily distorted by focusing on the suffering of some of its notable victims and stressing the pain caused without a closer look at the causes. Nevertheless, this pain is symptomatic of the tremendous significance such practices have for the emerging ethos of twenty-first-century business. Much of what has been seen in the nineties gives a clear signal that stockholder capitalism is winning out over stakeholder capitalism. That is to say, it is reasonable to fear that return on investment to stockholders may trump all other considerations, including employee wages and security, community well-being, and so on.

One telltale sign of this stockholder bias is in the way Wall Street has reacted to layoffs. Alan Downs, a veteran of downsizing procedures and author of *Corporate Executions*,[8] points out that an announcement of major layoffs generally sends stock prices up almost immediately. Investors are attracted to reductions in payroll, which many regard as the most significant ongoing liability of any company. In 1993, three large corporations—Boeing, IBM, and United Technologies—realized a rise in stock price of more than 30 percent within six to eight months of laying off between 10,500 (United Technologies) and 60,000 (IBM) employees (Downs, 14).

Not only do shareholders react favorably to the announcement of layoffs, they sometimes pressure management to pursue that strategy. The most common tactic is to insist that management negotiate lower wages or lay off workers to create a spike in earnings and a higher payment in dividends. Thus, the board of directors at Eastman Kodak fired its former CEO, Kay R. Whitmore, not because the company wasn't making money, but because he refused to downsize in response to lower revenues. Since then, the new CEO has laid off thousands of workers (Downs, 30).

Reasons given for layoffs are stated in terms other than simply bolstering stock values, of course. They vary from the need to be "lean and mean" or "flexible" in the face of competition to the claim that the company just doesn't have the funds to keep all employees on the payroll. Although some of these are bogus claims, there are legitimate reasons for downsizing. Global competition, technological change, and obsolete workforces are just a few. In fact, a number of large firms have used downsizing to buy time to get out from under some of these exigencies (Downs, 10–11). In certain instances, the elimination of positions may save the company and the jobs of the majority. Though a more robust economy on the eve of the new millennium has seen *some* abatement of the downsizing phenomenon of our decade, downsizing continues. More importantly, the pressures of globalization and technological change that lie behind many of these cutbacks remain and will doubtless increase.

In many cases, the decision to cut is simply the path of least resistance or a way to increase profits in an already profitable operation. In July of 1999 Eastman Kodak announced the elimination of 2,500 jobs as a step in the process of cutting 7,500 jobs, 1,200 more than it had announced in 1997. Kodak had had a 9 percent increase in earnings in the second quarter of 1998 but felt the cost savings were still necessary to insure greater profitability and preeminence in the market.[9] It may be argued that such downsizing, even in profitable times, is prudent and far-sighted. However, one cannot forget the costs to its victims. As the opening illustration from the *Times* article suggests, downsizing is particularly hard on older workers, who are often the prime targets for layoffs. Alan Downs quotes Irving S. Shapiro, chairman and CEO of Du Pont, on this very point: "If I were to weep for anybody today, I would weep for the middle-level people. If an employer has a choice of someone three years out of business school or someone age 50, which will they select? I'm afraid the job goes to the younger person" (Downs, 127). For people over fifty who find themselves out of a job, it is extremely difficult to find new positions at the same level of earnings they enjoyed in their former employment.

Sometimes companies go to considerable lengths to purge the payroll of senior workers. Take the story of Jonathan Kellet. Since graduating from college thirty years earlier, Jonathan worked his way up to regional vice president in an insurance company. One day, he and the other vice presidents were told that their primary task was to hire new sales managers. They would have to meet an assigned quota of successful new hires, and final hiring decisions would have to pass through headquarters. After a year's time, none of the VPs had met their quotas. They could not get their people approved for hiring by headquarters. All then came under pressure to take early retirement or a demotion. By inventing an impossible assignment, the head office had provided the basis for thinning the ranks (Downs, 130–32).

Even employees who remain after restructuring may feel as if they have suffered. Survivors frequently find that work life has become more difficult because they are expected to pick up a much larger load, and to do so while living with the stress of vulnerability and feelings of guilt over having survived.

Not long ago, I accepted an invitation to speak at a monthly dinner meeting of an association of health care professionals based at a corporate-owned hospital. A week before the scheduled event, the person who invited me called to express her regret that the dinner meeting had been canceled and that no further programs were being planned anytime soon. She went on to explain that since the corporate takeover of the hospital and subsequent downsizing the staff felt overworked and stressed. They no longer had the will or energy to continue their association meetings and activities. Not only does making the organization "lean and mean" result in fewer people sharing the wealth, it can also mean that shared values and relationships are dissipated.

A study just published adds another dimension to this picture of how downsizing affects those who remain. The researchers report that the workers interviewed stated that because of downsizing and other corporate changes they felt under pressure to do whatever was necessary to meet company goals, even if it meant unethical practices.[10]

More than one irony is associated with this pattern of downsizing that has marked business life, large and small, in the nineties. The first, downsizing doesn't often work. As a Wyatt and Company survey of more than a thousand corporations that had initiated downsizing programs found (Downs, 11–12),

- One-third said the profits increased as much as they expected after the layoff. (In other words, initial increases, which often prompted downsizing, did not prove to be sustainable.)
- Fewer than half said that their cuts had reduced expenses as much as expected over time—an understandable result, consid-

ering that four out of five managers reported rehiring for the eliminated positions.

- A small minority reported a satisfactory increase in shareholders' return on investment as a result of the layoff.

Parenthetically, we need to say that, while we can be grateful for the rehiring brought about by the failure of downsizing and, more recently by the upturn in the economy, that does not represent a reversal in every respect. Many still remain displaced and in lower paying jobs. All positions have not been restored and all wounds have not been healed. More importantly, the peak years of downsizing in the nineties remind us of how vulnerable people can be both to greed for profit and the poor managerial judgment that can accompany it. Furthermore, the uptick in prosperity and employment opportunities can tempt us to reiterate our beliefs in unlimited opportunities and dismiss the pain of downsizing as momentary and inconsequential. *It is now in the economic good times at the beginning of our new millennium that we should be examining this phenomenon before it happens again.*

The second irony is that CEOs who order massive layoffs often reap huge financial benefits for "improving profit" when in some cases it was their poor management that created the need for cutbacks in the first place.[11]

## EXECUTIVE COMPENSATION: "IN SEARCH OF EXCESS"

Graef S. Crystal's much-discussed 1991 book, *In Search of Excess,* maps the terrain of executive overcompensation in American business. Though his research is now close to a decade old, more recent reports indicate that the practices he unveiled are still common.

America's materialism, combined with its individualism and appreciation for those who have "made it," have helped to create an ethos of virtually unlimited financial rewards for those who can prove their worth in the compensation marketplace. The sense that there might be a limit to what anyone is worth in a business organization—J. P. Morgan, in the nineteenth century, believed that no executive should make more than twenty times the pay of the lowest worker—has apparently been set aside as a quaint idea. In terms of real income, dollars adjusted to inflation, manufacturing workers' wages remained flat during the seventies and eighties while CEO salaries increased threefold. In 1974, the typical CEO earned thirty-five times the pay of the average manufacturing worker. By the nineties, that number has jumped to 120 to 150 times the pay of the average worker.[12] Those figures have now been eclipsed at the end of the nineties. The frequently cited figure in 1999 is that CEO compensation is 419 times that of the average line worker.[13]

Crystal writes: "A 1991 study I undertook for *Fortune* showed that 86 percent of the CEOs among 200 major companies (the top 100 industrials, the top 50 diversified service companies, and the top 10 from each of the listings for commercial banks, diversified financial institutions, retailers, transportation companies and utilities) earned $1 million or more per year, while the average CEO earned $1.4 million per year in base salary and annual bonus, and $2.8 million per year when the value of long-term incentives such as stock options was figured in."[14] Of course, these are just averages. There are notable cases in which executive compensation exceeds that norm of excess.

While individualism and an appreciation for merit or material success are the driving cultural forces in the dramatically high levels of executive compensation, the fact is, compensation and performance don't always match. Thus, Crystal's chapter entitled "High Pay, Low Performance" details case after case of executives who raked in huge pay packages while failing reasonable tests of CEO performance.[15]

As a 1997 *Business Week* article reads, "the beat goes on." The author comments, "the staggering rise in pay for the good, the bad, and the indifferent has left even some advocates of pay for performance wondering whether the balance between the CEO and shareholder is tilting the wrong way" when someone like H.J. Heinz's CEO received $64.2 million while his company lost ground to competitors and in the stock market. Such developments prompted this remark by leadership guru Warren Bennis: "Performance criteria are almost like intellectual Silly Putty."[16]

If we need another example, we have one that was made public in March of 1999. After a fourth quarter in which Citigroup Inc. lost 27 percent in earnings, they awarded their co-chairmen, John S. Reed and Sanford I. Weill, compensation and stock options of $26.4 million and $27.2 million respectively. With a quick glance back to our previous section, the article about their pay package also reported that Citigroup has announced thousands of job cuts.[17]

Even conservative Catholic theologian Michael Novak, a consistent apologist for democratic capitalism, finds himself forced to recognize the problem of excessive compensation. He is clear that he is no advocate of absolute equality, except under the law. "Yet, observation shows that business executives are blind to the social destructiveness of current levels of compensation. Current practices give the appearance of cozy collusion, in which executives on one another's governing boards scratch each other's backs, heedless of the sacrifices others in their firms are making. For the sake of the moral reputation of business, executive belt tightening is desperately needed, and moral leadership from somewhere in business must step forward."[18]

Indeed, the offense created by excessive wealth at the expense of others, which Novak at least senses, even threatens to erode the tolerance for greed. As Peter Drucker, an illumine in the field of management education, has warned, "Few top executives can even imagine the hatred, contempt and fury that has been created, not primarily among blue-collar workers who never had an exalted opinion of their 'bosses,' but among their middle management and professional people. I don't know what form it will take, but the envy developing from their enormous wealth will cause trouble."[19]

It will be interesting to see how prophetic Drucker will turn out to be. The degree to which things are financially "out of whack" escapes no one's attention, even those in the mainstream of the American way of business. A textbook on business and society, widely used in business schools across the country, raises this salient point at the very beginning of the text: "A 1996 report by the Organization for Economic Cooperation and Development (OECD) determined the United States had the most unequal distribution of wealth among the advanced industrialized nations."[20]

In a similar vein, the venerable *Harvard Business Review* recently published an article with the provocative title "Toward an Apartheid Economy?" The opening sentences set the tone:

> Rising inequality. Stagnant real wages. A declining middle class. High levels of child poverty. Insecure workers. A waning union movement. Homeless people in every city. Bursting jails and prisons. A fraying social safety net. Does that sound like a third-world economy heading toward disaster? Or, perhaps a neo-Marxian vision of the future of

capitalism? Or is it a description of the United States moving into the twenty-first century?[21]

The article goes on to provide statistical grounding for this evidence of our growing inequality as a society—showing how we lag behind our counterparts in the developed world when it comes to the basic well-being of the average person and analyzing the social consequences of inequality, namely, crime, job insecurity, stress on family life, and political turmoil. "But the ultimate cost of increasing inequality," author Richard Freeman writes, "lies in the potential for an apartheid economy, one in which the rich live aloof in their exclusive suburbs and expensive apartments with little connection to the working poor in their slums."[22] Perhaps, he suggests, we are already blind to the plight of the less fortunate, as many whites were blind to the suffering of nonwhites in apartheid South Africa.

Certainly, those 43 million people in the United States without health insurance must feel as though they are largely unseen. On a global scale, residents of less-developed countries must also feel as though they are on the wrong end of an international apartheid economy. Both our national health care and the global economic order are now under the sway of market forces. This will be examined in the next two chapters, but for now, some theological reflection should pave the way for the discussion that will follow in those chapters.

## DIVINE ORDER AND ECONOMIC ORDER: FROM LUKE TO LUTHER

As explained in the previous chapter, the New Testament, and the Gospel of Luke in particular, critiques a world out of whack in which great disparities are created by a combination of individual avarice and systemic greed. Also mentioned, the disparity Luke had in his crosshairs tends to replay itself in different contexts and times. Developments charted in this chapter are surely yet another instance. Same song, new stanza.

Here it is worth sampling a bit more of Martin Luther's treatise, "Trade and Usury," as a reminder that some of the concerns of greed and justice in economic life are perennial. Luther attempts to help merchants, but he also criticizes some of their practices. He recognizes that, however morally ambivalent it may seem, commerce is here to stay and has a role to play. He realizes that determining exactly what is the right amount of profit is impossible, yet he stresses an obligation to avoid the excesses of greed. His formula for determining in good conscience an acceptable level of profit could readily serve as a wake-up call for those considering downsizing in order to spike profits in an already profitable operation. It could also serve as a model for determining executive compensation.

> In determining how much profit you ought to take on your business and your labor, there is no better way to reckon it than by computing the amount of time and labor you have put into it, and comparing that with the effort of a day laborer . . . and seeing how much he earns in a day. On that basis figure how many days you have spent in getting your wares and bringing them to your place of business and how much labor and risk was involved.[23]

What Luther was doing in his own, very different sixteenth-century environment is not so different from what I am attempting to do here. There, at the dawn of early capitalism, Luther spoke, not as an economist with a theory to advance, but as a Christian pastor concerned with justice in the marketplace. He was asking, as I am, doesn't faith give some guidance even in what are admittedly complex and often ambiguous circumstances of economic life?

Luther's theology provides other, more important resources for addressing issues of economic life. It is often thought that Luther's reform was largely individualistic in orientation and did not speak directly to social structure. The great Luther historian Karl Holl, however, has effectively argued that Luther's reform developed not only a new concept of personality but a new concept of community. It is a concept of community that "emphasizes not only the individual's duty of consideration and helpfulness to his neighbor but also the duty of the community as a whole to take care of those unable to work and to protect the weak from the strong."[24]

Of interest is the manner in which Luther's fundamental theology addresses human community, the very structure of our life together and how it is ordered. Chapter 1 described an offhand remark Luther made about a vanishing feudal order in which the rules of economic life favored the concentration of power in the hands of the nobles. However, the bulk of his thought moves in a very different direction. Far from being elitist in outlook, Luther was concerned for the plight of the poor and for the need of political and economic structures to serve the good of all.

In an interesting discussion, historian Carter Lindberg has noted the social significance of a little-known treatise of Luther's entitled "The Blessed Sacrament of the Holy and True Body of Christ, and the Brotherhoods." In attacking achievement-oriented piety, specifically, how it reflected a general orientation toward an egocentric striving for salvation, Luther completely overhauled the prevailing attitude toward poverty and Christian responsibility. Up to this time, it was thought that the poor existed in order that the saintly might do works of charity for their own spiritual reward. Concern for the plight of the poor was secondary to the profit of doing good works. By stressing the centrality and sufficiency of grace, and the unity of all in the sacrament of the Lord's Supper, Luther set Christians free from anxiety over works to care for their neighbors out of concern for them and their needs. His fundamental evangelical theology of the sacrament was, then, inseparable from his vision of a caring and sharing community.[25] The Reformation undid the spirituality of the late medieval period, which in effect had positioned the poor as recipients of charity, a classification that favored the wealthy.

Much of the strength of Luther's reform was his keen ability to name the demons that beset people in power. Chief among the demons was the manner in which the church burdened the consciences of its people with demands for works of obedience to churchly discipline. This fostered a bondage to fear instead of devotion to freedom and joy in knowing the promise of God's forgiveness and acceptance. Luther saw clearly that this coercive approach to spiritual life had its counterpart in the social sphere. The use of political power to enforce religious conformity and the use of ecclesiastical authority to gain political ends were all too common. It was in this context that Luther crafted his vision of God's two modes of rule—later to be dubbed his "two kingdoms" doctrine—as the foundation of a sociopolitical alternative.[26]

Luther taught that God rules the world according to two modes of sovereignty. God's left-hand mode of rule is expressed through the authorities, or "orders," God has established to ensure justice, peace, and the common good. These orders refer to the roles and relationships associated with the institutions of marriage, parenthood, government, and economic life. In and through these structures, God rules by what is often called the "civil use" of divine law. The force of law is needed to curb the negative forces of a sinful world, and faithful service in the context of these orders is required to promote positive social values. God's right-hand mode of rule is exerted through the gracious promise of the gospel, at work in the hearts of believers. God's left-hand rule establishes justice. God's right-hand rule instills and inspires love.

Luther called upon both secular and religious leaders to serve that expression of God's rule appropriate to their office and calling. He sought an end to the egregious abuses that occurred when these leaders stepped outside their proper spheres of authority. Although the two modes of God's rule were to be distinguished for the sake of good and just order, they were not to be separated in theory or in practice. It is not as though the religious community had no interest in secular matters, or that love and justice were somehow unrelated.[27]

To be sure, Luther's notion of "two kingdoms" was transformed by later generations of Lutherans into a dualistic formula that separated the mission of the church from concerns for societal reform. This "quietism" led to some glaring incidents in the history of Lutheranism in which the church turned a deaf ear to the cries of injustice.[28] Discussion of the way in which contemporary theology has transcended this dualism and breathed fresh new air into some of the basic insights of Luther's thought comes in the final chapter. For the present, it is sufficient to note that, despite some inconsistencies in thought, he rejected the tendencies in both the monastic tradition and the left wing of the Reformation to withdraw from civil life and its concerns. Certainly his bold confrontations with secular leaders made it clear that he was not one for cynical acceptance of the status quo, despite his considerable realism.[29]

Christians live under and serve both forms of God's rule at the same time. Their obedient response to God's twofold rule is the foundation of their participation in service to their neighbors. This includes not only concern for individuals but involvement in improving governmental, social, and economic institutions. Christians are driven by love in response to God's left-hand rule to seek justice in the so-called secular realm, just as they are driven by love in response to God's right-hand rule to go the extra mile for someone in need.

Here, then, is the crux of this discussion. Based on this Reformation pattern, Christians are encouraged to be constructively involved in the affairs of economic life. On the one hand, they will promote the capacity of business to serve the good of the human community and they will support the cultivation of justice and integrity in the conduct of business. On the other hand, Christians will feel free and empowered to speak critically and prophetically when business greed and abuse are harmful to the general good.

If business is indeed an integral part of the economic order and thus a part of the various orders God has established for the good of all creation, then business is in an interactive relationship with all other institutions of God's providential design. Economic institutions are not a law unto themselves. They don't travel in their own exclusive orbit.

Conscientious Christians will recognize, then, that there are times when, for example, government must limit the freedom and choices of business. In certain matters, such as health, safety, and environmental protection, there will always be need for regulation. However, there are also times when business needs to be free of government regulation. Whichever the case, the test will be which course of action contributes most to justice and the good of the whole, including the whole earth as well as the whole society of humankind. Likewise, business and government must work together to sustain the values of family life and human community, which are also among the orders begotten of God's providential love. Several things follow from these observations.

First, profitability in the economic order, though necessary for the survival of businesses, is a means to a larger end, not an end in itself. The purpose of business is to serve the well-being of all its stakeholders—employees and their families, communities, customers, the environment, and so on—not just the shareholders. That is, the interrelatedness of business with other orders of God's design clearly favors stakeholder capitalism over stockholder capitalism (a more complete discussion of this is in chapter 7).

Second, when the accounts of downsizing in America are reviewed, and their negative impact on so many different facets of life observed, the truth of business's interrelatedness with the values at stake in the other orders of life stands out. Because one purpose of Luther's "two kingdoms" doctrine was to preserve the integrity of God's left-hand rule institutions from inappropriate interference by ecclesiastical authorities, one might be tempted to argue that those institutions should be left alone. In other words, downsizing is simply a painful adjustment to market forces that shouldn't be the subject of Christian moral judgment. But, the inextricable relatedness of economic institutions to other social and political institutions, including their subordination to the purposes of God's rule of justice, puts into context the autonomy of business, making that argument difficult to sustain.

Third, it follows from the premise that God's providential love works through the left-hand rule of justice for the good of all that the burden of proof rests on decisions like downsizing, which have such dire and far-reaching ramifications. Taking that a step farther, layoffs not driven by the tragic necessity of organizational survival are morally wrong. And, when such moves are allied with huge pay benefits and return on investment for the few at the expense of the many, it is hard to see them as anything but greed. Luke's message and Luther's insights coalesce to reveal that something is seriously "out of whack."

It is certainly true that Christian moral judgment need always be seasoned with a sense of realism. Theological recognition that we live in a world fraught with ambiguity and uncertainty forces the realization that ethical choices are not always accompanied by clarity and certainty. Therefore, not all instances of downsizing are the same, morally speaking. Some are driven by ineluctable necessity while others emerge from honest, agonizing struggles with genuine uncertainties. But in those cases when downsizing does unnecessary and indefensible damage to individuals, families, and communities, realism demands seeing them for what they are, expressions of greed on the part of those in power.

Christians cannot excuse themselves from dealing with this judgment. They, too, live under the civil use of God's law, which they are called to interpret and uphold. Beyond that, however, Christians also see that in the compromise of those values, which the orders of God exist to serve, there is a compromise of neighbor love. Loving thy neighbor, engendered by God's rule through the grace of the Gospel, is the very love that energizes Christian commitment to justice.

In Reformation theology, the link between love and justice, the link that unites Christian response to both forms of God's rule, is often dealt with in the theology of "vocation." This is the place to examine one's calling in life in light of one's calling as a Christian. In a previous book on ethics in business, I suggest that our vocation as Christians should enable us to see an occupation as an avenue of service to others. Rather than the self-serving impulses so common in ambitious careerism, the call to be Christ's person should prompt self-giving.[30] This perspective's implications on executive compensation should be quite obvious.

Much more needs to be said about the theology of Christian calling as it pertains to Christian perspectives on economic life, greed, and sharing, and it will be in a later chapter. But for now, it is important to note that in the real world of business there are some genuine "good guys." There are concrete instances in which ethically responsible choices have been made instead of the greediest and most expedient alternative. Some companies have avoided the necessity of layoffs simply by allowing attrition to create the necessary reductions in workforce. And, going against the typical pattern of job elimination following a merger, when BB&T Financial Corporation and Southern National Corporation merged in 1995, they employed a hiring freeze to reduce the number of redundant positions in the new entity. As a result, they were able to save 95 percent of the jobs. "We have an obligation to take care of these people," said the chairman of BB&T, John Allison.[31]

Other companies, such as Hewlett-Packard, have reduced the number of hours employees work in order to get through tough times without resorting to layoffs. Early retirement packages that compensate for equity, which would otherwise be lost through early retirement, have also been able to ease the problem of workforce reduction. In 1992, Du Pont had considerable success with this approach.[32]

When reductions are inescapable, some firms have found creative ways to deal with them to minimize the impact on employees and communities. A case in point, the plan followed by British Petroleum (BP) in its decision to close an outmoded refinery at Llandarcy in South Wales. There were 750 jobs at stake, representing a sizeable portion of the small community's economy, which BP had essentially established when it built the refinery. Feeling a special sense of responsibility, the company instituted a number of measures, including a generous financial package for severance (more than what was required by law), immediate or deferred pensions for those employees close to retirement, alternative employment elsewhere in the company, and job search assistance. BP also established a separate company to redevelop the site. This new firm, operating with an endowment from the assets of the defunct refinery, set up a small business loan fund that led to the creation of seventy new businesses and more than five hundred jobs.[33]

Just as there are companies that find positive ways to deal with financial exigency other than immediate layoffs, so are there top executives who accept smaller paychecks in times of success. Graef Crystal, in a follow-up study to his book done for *U.S. News and World Report,* discovered some examples of executives who perform well but take relatively modest compensation. Topping that list is Warren Buffet, one of the most successful investors of all time. His actual salary from his company, Berkshire Hathaway, for the year investigated was $324,000. Salaries among his peers in competing firms exceeded 6 million. Additional members of this class include Steven Burd of Safeway, O.G. Richard of Columbia Gas, and John Perlegos of Atmel Corporation. These CEOS took anywhere from a tenth to an eighth of what their competitors raked in and all were in the high performance category.[34]

Such instances, however rare, are significant. They remind onlookers that the combination of competence and fairness are virtues of leadership that serve the whole organization.

## QUESTIONS FOR DISCUSSION

1. Does the phenomenon of downsizing contradict the American belief in limitless growth and opportunity? Does it suggest that the greed of some can limit the freedom and opportunity of others?
2. Many people justify their wealth by citing the ways in which they can use it to do good. When is this a legitimate claim and when might it be self-deceiving?
3. Can you think of instances when businesses and business leaders have made good faith efforts to protect the interests of all stakeholders, even in tough times?
4. We have spoken almost exclusively about the behavior of corporations and their leadership, yet most of the economy is driven by small business. In your experience, what are the similarities and differences when comparing small-business practices with those of corporations?

# 4

# UNSHARED GOODS: HEALTH CARE IN AMERICA

POET, WRITER, AND FRIEND OF NATURE Wendell Berry quotes Emerson: "I grasp the hands of those next to me, and take my place in the ring to suffer and to work, taught by an instinct, that so shall the dumb abyss be vocal with speech." It is a passage Berry believes voices the reality that living is a communal act. In Emerson's words, "we see how common work, common suffering, and a common willingness to join and belong are the conditions that make speech possible in 'the dumb abyss' in which we are divided," Berry writes.[1] "Communion," "communication," and "community" all belong to the same family. They entail one another. They are all implicit in the notion of "sharing."

Berry goes on to observe that regard for such a community of intimate mutual involvement has, lamentably, been largely neglected in American literature. Far more attention has been paid to the individual—whether heroic or beset by oppression, inner turmoil, or some combination of these. Often the individual, heroic or not, is depicted as the victim of community.[2] Certainly, literature is a reflector and shaper of culture. What it reflects and shapes in Berry's analysis is a preoccupation with the saga of the individual rather than the values of community. This is another face of the present project, which seeks appropriate expressions of community, a sharing society, and seeks to discern the culture of greed, in both its blatant and subtle systemic forms, which threatens that community and its common good.

In the first chapter I discussed our twin cultural impulses of placing personal freedom ahead of responsibility to community and of refusing to believe that there are limits to economic growth and the possibilities of having more of everything. I further suggested that these impulses embedded in our culture have enabled greed to flourish by giving individuals and individual groups a wide berth to pursue their fortunes, bolstered by the conviction that there is always more for those who want it or need it. In the next chapter, then, we saw how the biblical ideal of sharing stands in contrast to greed by recognizing the limits our neighbor's needs place upon our aspirations. The refusal of humanity to accept the limits inherent in its creation in the image of God and the turn away from God and the neighbor toward the self are at the heart of sin.

Greed hurts community. This is true when it is manifest in the ambitions of individuals or individual groups. It is also true when it finds expression in the stark inequalities of the very systems by which the goods of life are distributed. (When things are "out of whack.") The first of these two forms that greed takes was featured in the last chapter. The review of downsizing during the nineties, the growth of the income gap, and the runaway salaries of corporate executives provided a kind of case study on how greed affects business's various stakeholders.

In the present chapter we discuss issues of managed care and the problematic of universal health coverage. In the case of managed care, we have yet another instance of corporate greed exerting itself to the detriment of many of its stakeholders. Once again we have evidence that the interests of individuals and individual groups are trumping the needs of the community. (In this case it seems all the more poignant because the need is for quality health care, and the cost savings potential of managed care could have been directed to the benefit of the many rather than the profit of the few.) When we turn our attention to the question of universal health care coverage, the focus shifts from the greed of individuals or corporations to the way in which the culturally embedded drive for more and our reluctance to limit choices get in the way of our own best interests and result in terrible disparities in sharing the good of health care. Greed in this de facto systemic form is all the more insidious because individuals do not recognize their own complicity.

## HEALTH CARE IN AMERICA

- A mother of a child with leukemia wants the child's pediatrician to decide what care her child needs, but her managed care organization (MCO) makes this determination.

- A man suffering from severe pain drives to the closest hospital thinking he is having a heart attack. He learns the hospital does not participate in the health plan. He finds that he must pay more because he did not get preapproval to go to the emergency room. When he learns that it was not a heart attack after all, he is told he must pay the entire cost. Under the guidelines of his MCO, severe pain does not justify an emergency room visit.
- A child with cancer needs to see a pediatric oncologist. Her health plan has only an adult oncologist on staff and does not allow members to go outside the plan.

These cases are from a legislative alert sent out to mobilize support for a national patient's rights bill to assist people in contending with such problems in the now ubiquitous managed health care system in the United States. They are indicative of the types of problems people under managed plans face, and fear. Such instances are fodder for growing public concern over the consequences of having placed the health care delivery system in the hands of corporate structures through the introduction of managed care organizations. More than half the people surveyed in a recent Harris poll believe the trend toward managed care is harmful to the quality of medical services.[3] The first attempt at a patient's rights bill failed, but a strong bipartisan bill passed the House in October of 1999 and is presently in conference committee facing off with a considerably weaker Senate version. A long list of patient protections in the House bill, including quality care guarantees and provisions to hold managed care companies accountable, reflects the growing insistence of the public that patients be placed above profits. Moreover, since early 1997, twenty-seven states have adopted patient protection laws.[4] Before delving further into these concerns, it might be helpful to put the development of managed care into a brief historical perspective.

## THE MOVE TO MANAGED CARE

It is a relatively recent development in the history of medicine that the populace has felt, almost unanimously, that one is better off having medical care than not. To be sure, the practice of medicine has always been respected and sought, but confidence in its ability to meet most of the challenges of disease and disaster is a twentieth-century phenomenon. Dramatic medical success during the twentieth century—miracle drugs, vaccines, daring new surgical procedures, transplants, sophisticated diagnostic techniques, and so on—has created an unprecedented demand for access to medical care.

It is no accident, then, that the rise of third-party payers (private and governmental) has occurred more or less simultaneously with the development of more and more effective medicine. When medicine was an uncertain blessing, notwithstanding the dedicated service of doctors and nurses, people paid for medical services directly out of their own pocket. But as medical care became more effective, it became more elaborate and more expensive. The development of third-party payers was almost an inevitable response to a growing demand.

The developing mythology of an omnicompetent medical profession and the desire for medical services soon led to the position that access to medical care is not only a good thing but a need and a right. This national mentality will be revisited as the discussion proceeds. For now, it is enough to note that this conviction, coupled with the fact that medical costs were rising at astounding rates, led to a number of initiatives in the 1960s to establish a national health care program of universal coverage. At least five different bills were being discussed in Congress during that decade. "Healthcare for All Americans," backed by organized labor and a broad political coalition, seemed the most comprehensive, if memory serves. At the time, it seemed certain that universal health care coverage would be enacted; the only question was what form it would take.

For those who held to that assumption, there was to be a rude awakening. The first bills for the salad days of Medicare came rolling in. The tab seemed unaffordable without serious cost-containment measures. The spiraling costs of medical care, which in part prompted the quest to provide national health care, stood in the way of getting legislation passed. During the two decades of the fifties and sixties medical costs rose by 400 percent. A variety of unnecessary procedures were performed, and little attention was paid to preventative medicine.[5]

While the public and the medical profession debated alternative ways to deliver health care, which may have promoted the cost containment necessary, and what constituted "basic health care coverage" for everyone (a health care floor, if you will), by the seventies, the mood shifted to interest in preventative medicine and public health initiatives such as sanitation and inoculation. Cognizant of the fact that the biggest gains in health and life expectancy have historically come from public health measures and technological gains, such as refrigeration, public policy makers were working to redirect consciousness from "sick care" to staying healthy. Public campaigns against smoking, high-cholesterol diets, and alcohol abuse were paired with encouragement to exercise and "buckle up" in an effort to get Americans to take more responsibility for their own health.

The trend toward managed care is probably best understood against this brief historical backdrop. If physicians under the previous fee-for-service/third-party payer systems ran up costs by doing too many tests and "unnecessary" procedures, managed care has corrected this by replacing fee for service with capitation or some similar arrangement giving physicians incentives to keep costs down. If patients and physicians alike became addicted to the costly reliance on "sick care," managed care provides a system that encourages people to maintain their own health and rewards them for doing so by making it financially disadvantageous to get sick.

While many complain that the burgeoning growth of medical technology has led to a costly and unnecessary proliferation and duplication of these services and technologies (every hospital does not have to have all the latest technology for all kinds of conditions or all the latest diagnostic and treatment services for all kinds of conditions), managed care has shown the way toward streamlining the system. At its best, managed care is able to improve care and save money by linking hospitals, doctors, and specialists, and by utilizing shared electronic records and treatment protocols.[6]

However, the fear is that the pendulum has swung too far in the direction of managed care. Physicians and other health care professionals frequently feel serious pressures to control costs and abide by practice standards and guidelines that limit the use of resources when benefits are expected to be marginal relative to costs. "These rules and standards may at times be at odds with what the patient wants, and even what the practitioner judges to be in the patient's best interests."[7] It is not difficult to understand why some worry that both physicians and patients can easily be regarded as factors in an economic equation rather than persons engaged in a sacred covenant.

Distinguished physician Christine Cassell , writing in the *Annals of Internal Medicine* several years ago, issued this warning out of her expressed concern for the soul of medicine: "Accepting the 'business' paradigm especially in a profit-centered corporate setting, turns people away from concern for the patient toward concern for the bottom line."[8] The problem, says Cassell, is not managed care per se, but profit.

Dr. Cassell was reflecting upon a common fear among a number of her colleagues who joined her in signing a statement entitled the "Patient-Physician Covenant," which reads in part:

> Today this covenant of trust [between patient and physician] is significantly threatened. From within there is a growing legitimation of the physician's materialistic self-interest; from without, for-profit forces press the physician into the role of commercial agent to enhance the profitability of health care organizations.[9]

More than three thousand physicians from Massachusetts echoed this manifesto by signing one of their own, entitled "For Our Patients, Not for Profits."[10] Concern has also led a growing number of physicians to refuse to deal with managed care organizations whose policies they feel are incompatible with integrity in the practice of medicine. My own family practice group did just that. Shortly after their decision, there were reports in other cities of significant defections from the same insurance carrier. More disturbing, a recent poll by the Tufts School of Medicine found that 70 percent of physicians surveyed reported exaggerating patient symptoms to prevent premature release from the hospital by their health maintenance organizations.[11]

There is no question that managed care plans work well for many, especially those who are reasonably healthy and those who benefit from coordinated care. But there are many who feel underserved, many who are denied essential treatments because of some financially based provision in their coverage.

Adding fuel to the fire are reports of huge salaries paid to the corporate executives who run managed care organizations. We seem to be hearing echoes here of the general problem of excessive executive compensation discussed in the last chapter. In fact, the comparison is striking when we consider that many of the health maintenance organizations (HMOs), so prominent as a vehicle of managed care, have been financially troubled at the very time their CEOs have taken home big bucks. A 1997 sample of salaries yielded the following figures for chief executives. Steve Wiggins of Oxford Health Plans, Inc., made $30.7 million. This top salary was followed by

Wilson Taylor of Cigna at $12.4 million, William McGuire of United Health Care at $8.6 million, Gregory Wolfe of Humana, Inc., at $2.9 million, and Alan Hoops of PacifiCare Health Systems at a mere $1.7 million. In addition to these salaries each had unexercised stock options, valued at $20 million in one case and $61 million in another.[12] The clear impression one receives from this kind of data is that a very small number of the stakeholders in this system are actually benefiting and the few that are seem to profit from what is denied to others. Once again, we have another plausible example of how the interests of a few can detract from the needs of the many.

If top personnel are thriving but patients and profits are not, it's tempting to recall those children's book exercises that ask, What's wrong with this picture?

Health maintenance organizations' (HMOs') attempts since 1998 to get out of the business of covering the Medicare population has heightened suspicions that the financial considerations crowd out humane considerations all too readily. In the United States's privatized health care system, there are obvious financial disincentives to covering the sickest, most vulnerable segment of the population.[13]

Managed care has created some new opportunities for greed as well as new and distressing tension between financial gain and humane values. Nevertheless, managed care has provided some needed correctives. Streamlining the delivery system not simply to become more financially efficient but to in some cases improve care, reducing costs, and stressing preventative medicine are necessary steps to making health care coverage available to all. Indeed, managed care could be an essential vehicle for enabling universal coverage.

Unfortunately, the savings from managed care have not been directed toward expanded coverage. In some respects, the opposite is true. As MCOs use their financial leverage to negotiate favorable contracts with hospitals and other providers, those institutions find it less and less possible to generate sufficient income from paying clients to cover the needs of those who can't pay.[14]

Certainly, we should press some managed care organizations to keep the *care* of patients and the *management* of money in proper balance. We should be concerned about legislation that keeps them accountable for patient care. We should applaud when they take initiatives to place patient care and the doctor's judgment in the forefront as United Health Group did in November of 1999. United announced a change in policy that would now allow hospitalization and treatment decisions to be made by the patient's doctor without interference by the insurer.[15] However, in the final analysis, we have a larger problem. We have 43 million without health care insurance in our country. The fact that the appropriate cost savings of managed care are not being pumped into the resources for a system of universal health care is not the fault of managed care organizations per se. It is an issue for our society as a whole.

## UNIVERSAL COVERAGE AND THE CULTURE OF "MORE"

Daniel Callahan, a respected and accomplished thinker in the field of ethics in medicine, is also one of the most insightful when it comes to medicine in American culture. His work deserves examination here.

As suggested by the title of his 1987 book, *Setting Limits: Medical Goals in an Aging Society,* Callahan challenged American medicine and society to face the limits imposed by the aging population in the United States. He called upon Americans to exchange the preoccupation with prolonging life at all costs with the acceptance of a natural life span. Such a conversion could not only shift medical concentration from heroics to keep people alive under even the direst conditions to a focus on comfort care at the end of life, it could redirect the priorities of medicine to result in a better distribution of health care resources. Indeed, the cultural tendency in America to believe that medicine can hold back death indefinitely could be one of the reasons the health care system is "out of whack." The key is to recognize and set limits, but to succeed in doing that people must be ready to temper their individual demands for all the medical science they can lay their hands on. In other words, some kind of sharing is needed.[16]

In his latest book, *False Hopes,*[17] Callahan writes even more directly on the disparities in health care coverage. Callahan sees the development and use of modern medicine under the sway of the very cultural forces addressed here: the priority of individual freedom to the point of individualism and the persistent sense of limitlessness.

According to Callahan, the development of modern medicine in the United States has been driven by Americans putting self before community (Callahan, 44, 81, 160ff.). The aspirations of individuals to have more of the benefits of medical science and technology are coupled with the aspirations of medicine for endless progress. The result: more and more medicine. "When asked about the goals of the labor movement . . . Samuel Gompers [an early labor leader who helped found what later became the American Federation of Labor] is reputed to have said, 'More!' If modern medicine had a single collective voice it would probably say something like that; there is no ultimate end point, just *more* cure, *more* relief of suffering, *more* success in holding off death. . . . Precisely because modern medicine's unspoken goal is simply *more*, there are no limits to what can be hoped for and sought" (Callahan, 52).

The insatiable quest for more almost guarantees that multitudes will continue to be uninsured or underinsured. The runaway costs of medical progress according to the gospel of "more" will simply place it out of reach for a growing minority and leave it in the hands of those who have the money to consume medicine at a pace that fuels its own expansion.

Callahan argues that the societal idea that medicine should seek to satisfy virtually every individual need or desire and pursue every research possibility should be abandoned. Instead, people need to think in terms of *sustainability*, a term borrowed from the environmental movement. A sustainable environmental policy limits consumption so that all life may flourish in the present and in the future. Likewise, sustainable medicine recognizes the need to limit aspirations for progress so that affordable, sufficient health care can be equitably distributed among all people (Callahan, 33–36).

Sustainability does not come without difficulty and tension, however. Callahan lays out three requirements for sustainable medicine, which present a clear challenge to present beliefs and attitudes.

The first requirement is learning to live within the boundaries of nature, which is to say, respecting the natural life cycle. Applied to the realm of health care, this ecological perspective is a logical companion to Callahan's appropriation of sustainability as a new ethos of medicine. Respecting the natural life cycle means being satisfied with the normal life span of seventy-five to eighty-two years in developed countries. Callahan suggests that this is generally satisfactory for most people to lead a full life (Callahan, 130–36).

The second requirement is for medicine to gear its idea of progress to dealing with the necessary struggle against nature within the natural life cycle, instead of continually trying to transcend our finitude. Costly life-sustaining measures at the end stages of life and medical research to extend life span are not the only expenses in medical progress; dollars must be generated to deal with the social costs of an aging society. For example, extending life through medical treatment means greater need for long-term care and a higher instance of dementia. Medical "progress" is necessary because nature is not benign. Disease and suffering must be dealt with. But Callahan posits the notion that progress needs to be mediated by a sense of the "aggregate impact of progress," meaning progress not just for one or a few, or in one area or another; it is overall progress for all people. Such a view of progress would help meet the third requirement, a sustainable medical economy, one with a more equitable distribution of health care for all people (Callahan, 136–38). Sustainability as the foundation of equitable distribution is a project that recognizes the interconnectedness of things; it is communal rather than individualistic in character.

It is not surprising, then, that a suitable companion for sustainability is the social virtue of solidarity. Solidarity is the ethos of a community united for the health and well-being of all. In solidarity, the freedom and rights of each individual to seek and demand more and more of medicine, and medicine's ambitious willingness to feed off those demands, are sublimated. A society ready to take responsibility for one another in education, economic life, security, and mutual respect is the kind of society in which sustainable medicine, equitably distributed, can flourish. It is a place where limits of growth and possibility in some areas are accepted for the greater good of all. It is a society in which personal responsibility for one's own health is an obligation owed to one's neighbors, a place where public health is considered the best collective progress in health (Callahan, 42–43, 154, 160–72).

Callahan is not without his critics, of course. Many would say that the notion of a natural life cycle is arbitrary; individual cases differ dramatically. How could one in good conscience deny certain medical procedures that can truly help simply because they are not the norm for a person over a certain age? Wouldn't it come to that kind of rationing? Furthermore, in order to buy his overall argument, one must be ready to accept his conviction that there is a natural life span that cannot be extended much beyond the life span currently enjoyed by people in developed countries. Many are by no means ready to concede that. Indeed, I suspect that current genetic research will fuel new hopes of ways to deal with disease and aging. Finally, others might well argue that placing limits on medical science or science in general is not in the long-term best interests of humankind. We can't stop scientific research just because we haven't adequately cared for everyone. In the long run, research discoveries will end up benefiting everyone.

It is important to recognize, as Callahan does, that seemingly greedy impulses for unlimited access to and unlimited progress for medicine are mingled with sincere and noble desires to fight disease and relieve suffering. Nonetheless, the challenge remains. Are we willing as individuals, consumers and practitioners, to limit our demands upon the resources of the health care system if it means that the public funds going into health care can be redirected to provide essential basic coverage for all? For now, it is enough to note that those features of managed care that are clearly lamentable, combined with the fact that 43 million people in the world's richest country have no health insurance, signal a system dreadfully "out of whack."

## WE DO NOT LIVE "BY LIFE ALONE"

This paraphrasing of Jesus' statement that we do not live by bread alone originated with ethicist Harmon Smith.[18] His point was that Christians should understand that personal life is more than bodily life. Our creation in the image of God and our hope in the resurrection teach us to value the body as God's good creation, but also to recognize that the fullness of life is in our relationship with God and our hope for the world to come. Desperate, heroic efforts in medicine to keep the body going at all costs may at times be a contradiction to these central convictions of the Christian faith.

Jesus' original statement comes in the context of his temptation in the wilderness, as recorded in Matthew 4. It is the first of the temptations. The devil wants Jesus to succumb to the allure of prosperity through the use of his divine power. To this Satan adds the further temptations of safety, or security, and worldly power. One can make a good case that these are the temptations of greed. Just as greed for bread, wealth, and other forms of material security and power becomes idolatrous, so clinging to life at all costs can be idolatrous.

It is conceivable that there are some forms of idolatry that are not greedy in outlook, but it also seems clear that greed can veer into idolatry when the object of individual desire becomes one's ultimate concern. To make a god of one's own lust for life blinds one to life with God and the community of life for which God has created and redeemed his people.

This supports Callahan's view that we need to accept a natural life span and curb our lust for extending life through more and more medicine. It is not difficult to imagine Christians nodding in assent to Callahan's proposal. It seems to resonate well with a faith grounded in the promise of the resurrection. It also resonates well with a faith grounded in the cross. The cross reflects the brokenness of humankind and warns against prideful assaults on mortality and against the dangers of ignoring human perversity.

But baptizing Callahan's arguments is not the mission here. Looking at the issues he raises through the prism of the Christian faith is. Doing so has unearthed some of the practical implications for health care policy of a life lived in the hope of God's promised future. This, then, opens the door to revisit a familiar theme.

## A PEOPLE OF ANTICIPATION—REPRISE

The end of chapter 2 spoke of the Christian community as a people of anticipation. It is an eschatological theme, a theme of hope and expectation for the coming of God's future reign. That dominion, revealed and sealed by Christ's victory over death, holds out the promise of life's triumph over death, but it doesn't stop there: wholeness will supplant decay throughout the entire creation.

The hope of the future is not for a heaven apart, a spiritual reality that succeeds the creation. It is a hope for a new creation in which all things are made whole in unity and harmony. The materiality of God's promises for humankind and the whole created order prompts us to be concerned for the conditions that afflict our neighbors and our environment. The protection of life, the relief of suffering, the promotion of health and healing, the alleviation of hunger and poverty, the quest for freedom from oppression, the care of the earth—these are ways we anticipate God's future. That is, when we seek these things in the present, we bear witness to our hope for the future.

Christians have long been committed to the sanctity of life, health, and healing. In this they follow the pattern of Jesus, who in anticipation of his own victory over death and evil did works of healing and emancipation from sin and death. Hope for the future activates the pursuit of life and health in the present, but Christians also understand that it is only in the future hope of resurrection that humankind possesses the indestructible fullness of life and wholeness in unity with God. Living in perpetual hope, and understanding it as such, leads to several conclusions about the direction of Christian commitment in the matter of health care.

First, the promise of life and wholeness in the reign of God should prompt the recognition that the call to anticipate is a call to care for the health and life of all people here and now. This is punctuated by the fact that all people are equal in dignity before God: there is neither Jew nor Greek, male nor female, slave nor free (Galatians 3:28).

Second, that perpetual hope is planted in God's future domain brings to light the limits that still constrain humankind and the limitations of sin. Achieving equality will mean dealing with those limits by sharing, that is, creating policies that limit the freedom of some to take more than their share.

Third, hope of future should make Christians open to sharing with neighbors in the present. It is in faith in the hope of God's promise that Christians entrust their lives to God and remain ever open to his calling. It is trust in God's merciful promise in Christ that sets Christians free from self-concern, free to love and serve God and their neighbors. This freedom is what Luther joyfully related in his *A Treatise on Christian Liberty.* "Behold, from faith thus flow forth love and joy in the Lord, and from love a joyful, willing, and free mind that serves one's neighbor willingly and takes no account of gratitude or ingratitude, of praise or blame, of gain or loss."[19]

This freedom in the trust of faith and hope stands in direct contrast to the drive for security, a quest to hold on to something in the present as a hedge against future threat and uncertainty. This was what the rich fool sought to do, and it stood in the way of sharing his prosperity. Faith and hope, open to the needs of one's neighbors and capable of love, constitute trust in God's promise rather than fear of the unknown.[20]

Clearly, the failure to establish a national system of universal health care coverage is largely due to the fear of various interest groups and certain chunks of the electorate that such a system will be contrary to their best interests. The drive for security, a hedge against the perceived threats of change, has proven more powerful than appeals for the needs of all citizens in the United States. Until a moral commitment to health care for all people is made, despite the difficulties and adjustments that will entail, the number of uninsured Americans will likely continue to grow.

Christians can appreciate the fact that any system of universal health care coverage will be imperfect and subject to conflicting claims. Theirs is a world of looking to—anticipating—the future. But Christians also have the courage of freedom in faith and hope to seek what love demands commitment to the care of all. Christians are realists and idealists at one and the same time! Out of our own hope we should be working to provide hope for those who have been left out.

Finally, the Christian community, as the community of anticipation, has a special call to advocacy for the poor. These people of anticipation are to understand their ethical vocation as a witness to the promises of God's future. As demonstrated by the parable of the rich man and Lazarus, in God's final reign, the inequities and disparities of the present will be set right. Addressing the inequities of our time is, then, our calling.

In the present context, the poor are not only those who are uninsured or underinsured; they include those cultural and ethnic groups vulnerable to injustice. Catholic ethicist Philip S. Keane, in his vision of a just system of adequate coverage for all, argues that justice demands that the basic standard of health care be the same for all. This means adequate health care coverage for everyone. For the vast majority of the poor who are marginalized by prejudice, lack of education, problems of access, and so on, however, special efforts will be required to enable their participation.[21] For Keane, those efforts entail the sharing of power. That is, the poor need not only health care, they need to be empowered to make full use of it.

It may be useful to entertain one more comment from Callahan. In his account of the current health care system in the United States, he characterized his own attempt to describe the consciousness of medicine and its consumers in this way: "The analogy I want to draw is between medicine's modern pursuit of unlimited progress and the pursuit, by global and local industry, of unlimited economic growth and affluence."[22] This statement underscores the connection between issues of health care and the issues of business and avarice in the previous chapter and is also a good transition to the next chapter. Hunger, health, and the global economy are inextricably intertwined. The issues we encounter when we look at economic life on a global scale and its impact on the quality of life bear a strong family resemblance to the issues we have already met.

## QUESTIONS FOR DISCUSSION

1. How can the benefits of managed care be blended with a commitment to provide universal coverage? What are the barriers that stand in the way? Are practical difficulties so great that the ideal must be given up?
2. Callahan insists that we must settle for a natural life span and set aside the extreme and expensive efforts to extend life at any cost. Such a view is more easily talked about in a general discussion than at the bedside of a dying loved one. What do you think about Callahan's proposal?
3. If health care is to be rationed to spread it around more equitably, what do you think about doing expensive eye surgery and laser treatment to sustain the sight of an eighty-eight-year-old person of sound mind and reasonable health?
4. It is easy to recognize greed for money, power, and resources among business and professional people in the health care industry. However, is it possible to speak of individuals or even the majority of a society as being "greedy" for health and life?

# 5
# UNSHARED GOODS: HUNGER AND THE GLOBAL ECONOMY

EARLIER THIS YEAR, I WAS PRIVILEGED TO DELIVER a lecture to some of the students and faculty at the University of Nairobi in Kenya, East Africa. The subject of the presentations was the theological foundation for the church's social witness. I tried to make a strong case that the central affirmations of the Christian faith commit the church to being an advocate for justice in the world. During the question-and-answer session that followed, a woman on the faculty asked, "If the church's faith commits it to seeking justice, why has it so often taken the side of the powerful?"

It was a disconcerting question. Of course, I have heard the issue raised many times before in various discussions. I have also seen it discussed extensively in print. Anyone who has had a basic course in church history has been made aware of instances that support the good professor's accusation. Liberation theologians in our own time have made the case forcefully.

On this occasion, her question struck home with peculiar urgency, and lingered well beyond the moment of my response. For two reasons, I think. First, the question was posed by a person in a country with firsthand experience of what it means to live outside the orbit of the powerful. And, second, it was posed to a person who does not see himself as among the powerful of this world. To deal with the issues of the church's conduct and one's own complicity in the arena of academic discourse or peer group debate is one thing. To deal with it face-to-face is really quite another. Such an arena gives the query a certain inescapability. One cannot simply theorize and theologize at a distance. Also, one wonders, by the sheer fact that the question was asked, whether the fine theological webs spun on behalf of social justice have simply been ineffectual in the church.

However, we need also to recognize that distinctions must be drawn between Christ and his people, and instances where the church has stood with the powerless and the poor need also to be lifted up. If, trusting in the grace of God, we can move beyond—not dismiss—the guilt of complicity and the fear of futility, both of which the professor's question evokes, another question awaits: How do we know with certainty what choices benefit the poor and which end up playing into the hands of the powerful? It is difficult to know where to step in the minefield of such an extraordinarily complex global political and economic situation. Nevertheless, there is no standing still.

## GLOBAL ECONOMY AND GLOBAL COMMUNITY

If the engines of economic life are not driven by some sense of communal caring or responsibility for one another, then greed, individual and systemic, proceeds unabated and disparities are increased. Economic life does not run on a separate track from all other activities and institutions. It is tightly woven together with the other "orders" of life, to recall Luther's term.

The idea that economics runs according to its own laws, independent of other considerations and subject to the corrections of Adam Smith's "invisible hand," has produced the notion of amoral business. But amorality, neither moral nor immoral, can be attributed only if business is understood as an economic institution divorced from community, for it is in the relational life of community that morality has its meaning. Even conservative business ethicists committed to the free enterprise system have rejected this idea, calling it the "myth of amoral business."[1]

In its 1992 study, *Christian Faith and the World Economy Today*, the World Council of Churches notes that the original meaning of *oikonomia*, the Greek origin of *economics*, refers to the management of a household. The suggestion is clear: economics is deeply enmeshed in communal relationships. Thus, the report continues, "'Economics' is by no means a separate part of reality on its own; rather it is one way of considering large complexes of social and community realities. . . . Again and again it is evident that 'economic problems' have to do with increasingly inescapable interdependence in the context of glaring inequalities of power."[2] Such "glaring inequalities" in global economic life strongly suggest that a community of values and mutual responsibility has developed at nothing like the pace of the global economy.

Advocates of economic globalization often argue that it will promote global community and eventually benefit everyone. However, the rapidly expanding global economy is an ambivalent phenomenon. It has the potential to expand materialism, further threaten the sustainability of the environment, and provide new avenues for greed that exacerbate the problems of injustice and multiply the possibilities of division and strife. At the same time, it can raise the standard of living for countless numbers of people and be a catalyst for global community—even justice—as market forces stimulate a greater sense of mutuality among nations. Perhaps the resolution to this ambivalence, then, is to direct that expansion toward a global community that can shape the global economy rather than expecting the economy to generate global community.[3]

Something of this concern for the priority of community over economy was expressed in an August 25, 1998, public letter from Leon F. Spencer, executive director of the ecumenical organization Washington Office on Africa. He was commenting on the Africa Growth and Opportunity Act, specifically, that it would commit African nations to a free market economy. Those provisions are not the issue, however. The real problem, Spencer writes, is "American insistence that African nations apply an economic perspective that within the United States is characterized by a striking absence of discussion about the common good." "A just policy toward Africa needs to affirm *community*, both in the sense of American and African commonalities and in the sense of respect for community needs and hopes within Africa." At the level of political action, this means quite simply an African trade policy that tries to be as attentive to the needs and prospects of Africa as it does to the opportunities for American business. This challenge underlies the essence of a wide variety of decisions in international economic life in which fairness and mutuality are at stake.

International business has begun to recognize the need to blend economic goals and values with humane goals and values. In 1994, a roundtable discussion held in Caux, Switzerland, brought together an impressive group of international business leaders who developed the Caux Principles. The seven principles, to which they committed their own organizations and which they urged upon other international business concerns, suggest that global community is indeed the force that shapes global economics.

The Caux signatories recognize, first of all, that business has a responsibility for the welfare of the communities in which it operates. In other words, it needs to be concerned for all stakeholders, not just shareholders. Other principles follow suit. The second, "orienting the effects of business toward innovation, justice and world community," takes into account the extraordinary power and influence of global business and the responsibility that goes with it to be a force for good. Principles supporting multilateral trade and respect for the environment punctuate the group's avowal of responsibility for justice and world community. Overall, the principles are an attempt to fuse the western values of human dignity and stakeholder rights with the Japanese notion of *kyosei*, "living and working together for the common good."[4]

If a global economy is to be shaped by the mutual responsibilities of a new sense of global community, then a global ethic is required to define those responsibilities. Essentially this is what the 1993 Parliament of the World's Religions has said. Delegates from across the world, representing virtually all the religions of the world, issued a declaration, "Toward a Global Ethic." The following excerpts from the section on solidarity and a just social order are particularly relevant to this discussion:[5]

> All over the world we find endless hunger, deficiency, and need. Not only individuals, but especially unjust institutions and structures are responsible for these tragedies. Millions of people are without work; millions are exploited by poor wage, forced to the edge of society, with their possibilities for the future destroyed. In many lands the gap between the poor and the rich, between the powerful and the powerless, is immense. We live in a world in which totalitarian state socialism as well as unbridled capitalism have hollowed out and destroyed many ethical and spiritual values. A materialistic mentality breeds greed for unlimited profit and a grasping for endless plunder. These demands claim more and more of the community's resources without obliging individuals to contribute more. The cancerous social evil of corruption thrives in the developing countries and in the developed countries alike.

To address this situation through a global ethic reflective of the great religious and ethical traditions of human kind, the parliament stated,

We must use economic and political power for *service to humanity* instead of misusing it in ruthless battles of domination. We must develop a spirit of compassion with those who suffer, with special care for the children, the aged, the poor, the disabled, the refugees, and the lonely.

We must cultivate *mutual respect* and consideration, so as to reach a reasonable balance of interests, instead of thinking only of unlimited power and unavoidable competitive struggles.

We must value a *sense of moderation and modesty* instead of an unquenchable need for money, prestige, and consumption! In greed humans lose their "soul," their freedom, their composure, their inner peace, and thus that which makes them human.

The parliament's declaration is noteworthy for its incisiveness and elegant witness to moral truth, but the most salient feature is that it does not lay the manifold evils of the world's injustices at the feet of a particular political or economic system. Instead, it zeroes in on the human spirit. Having the parliament's analysis and perspective in mind, as well as additional voices of advocacy and responsible business leadership to heed, it is time for another step. Perhaps it is time for a realm of global activity that will provide a barometer for how well globalization is working, its realities, problems, and possibilities.

## HUNGER AND THE GLOBAL ECONOMY

The phenomenon of globalization in its economic, political, cultural, and environmental dimensions is so vast that it staggers the mind. The matter of hunger, including economic and political activities associated with the production and distribution of food for the world's population, provides a good window through which to look at it. The 1998 Bread for the World Institute report, *Hunger in a Global Economy,*[6] provides an excellent resource. Like the parliament's declaration, it does not demonize systems but tries to analyze what works and what does not. The report does not make international business the fall guy, but calls upon it, as the Caux Principles have done, to be part of the solution. It pairs religious and moral insight with practical considerations. It helps make connections and it helps to find some directions. It makes clear that it will take the interaction—cooperative and coercive—of virtually all the forces at work in the emerging global community to bring about better and adequate sharing of the elemental good that is food and nutrition.

## CHARTING THE DISPARITIES

The institute's report provides extensive comparative statistics that draw a picture of the relative quality of life from country to country. There is no need here for an exhaustive analysis of these figures. It is sufficient to say that there was a strong and even obvious correlation between economic development, adequate food and nutrition, life expectancy, and education. For example, life expectancy in Sierra Leone was thirty-six for men and thirty-nine for women. The adult literacy rate was 43.7 percent for men and 16.7 percent for women. The recorded shortfall in the minimum required food supply was nearly 20 percent in 1992, and the per capita Gross National Product (GNP) was $180. By contrast, life expectancy in the Netherlands was seventy-five for men and nearly eighty-six for women. The adult literacy rate was 99 percent. There was no recorded shortfall in required food supply, and the per capita GNP was $24,000 (*Hunger in a Global Economy*, 92–109).

The contrast is striking with the comparison of two such countries, one very poor and the other prosperous. The correlations become even more significant and convincing looking at the statistics of El Salvador, a country not noted for its affluence that has progressed economically far beyond the level of Sierra Leone. In El Salvador, life expectancy was 66.5 for men and 72.5 for women. The adult literacy rate was 72.8 percent for males and 68.7 percent for females. The shortfall in food supply was only 4.1 percent and the per capita GNP was $1,610. While a poor country in economic terms when compared to one like the Netherlands, El Salvador's economic superiority to Sierra Leone ($1,610 per capita GNP versus $180 per capita GNP) puts it way ahead in health and education (*Hunger in a Global Economy*, 92–109).

Given these connections, and dozens more, detailed in the institute's report, it is not surprising to discover this statement: "The evidence is overwhelming that improving health and education among poor people, with a particular emphasis on gender equality and improved female literacy, contributes enormously to economic growth and poverty reduction" (*Hunger in a Global Economy*, 21). Of course, it follows that continued economic growth and poverty reduction will only improve education and health, assuming a stable and democratic political context.

## MANIFOLD CAUSES AND MANY-SIDED RESPONSES

Hunger is one face of inequality. Inequalities in economic opportunity go hand in hand with economic inequalities. Such inequalities of power include those related to political disenfranchisement; discrimination based on race, gender, or ethnicity; lack of public assistance; poor public health; and inadequate education. Such disparities in power seem to point to another phenomenon. Greed is the hoarding of power, as it is the hoarding of wealth. Those under its influence use their power to write the rules in favor of their own ambitions.

How in the world does one address these interlocking forces and their devastating impact on the health and well-being of millions? The Bread for the World Institute Report responded with its "Ten Ways to Make the World Economy Work Better for Hungry People" (*Hunger in a Global Economy*, 3).

1. Give priority to the needs of hungry and poor people when making economic decisions.
2. Complement markets with government and civic action to ensure secure livelihoods for all.
3. Include hungry and poor people in the decisions that affect their lives.
4. Coordinate policies among nations to foster full employment and other social goals.
5. Promote international trade—with safeguards for labor rights, the environment, and food security.
6. Foster food security through more liberal agricultural trade coupled with sound agricultural policies and safety nets.
7. Encourage responsible investing through policies that are good for businesses, workers, and consumers.
8. Focus the World Bank and other international financial institutions on reducing poverty, and make them accountable to the low-income communities they affect.
9. Relieve the debts of poor-country governments committed to reducing poverty, and expand foreign aid programs that help hungry and poor people.
10. Exercise our influence as responsible citizens, consumers, employers, workers, and investors to make the world economy work for everyone.

The report goes on to give each of these general principles far more detailed examination than can possibly be replicated here. One thing is plain from even a cursory look at the above list, however. The manifold inequalities of economic status and power that underlie hunger require a many-sided response from governments, economic institutions, civic and religious organizations, and individuals.

The fact that there are so many sides to possible solutions points to the difficulty of seeing all sides. Strong, democratic local government is essential to an effective, healthy national economy. Sometimes, however, what is done domestically may have unintended, unjust consequences. For example, ethicist and economist Daniel Finn, in his book *Just Trading,* has shown how agricultural price supports in the United States and Canada, originally designed to aid and preserve small rural farms and their communities, have misfired. Much of the money has gone to farmers who are far from struggling. The support has not, and really cannot, prop up the small rural economies for which it was intended. Thus, for example, it is estimated that consumers pay 104 percent more for milk than they would likely pay without subsidies. These higher prices then create a burden on the poor in the nations where subsidies are in place. At the same time, subsidies that are doled out on the basis of output are an incentive to overproduce. Farmers or the government, which sometimes holds their produce, have an excess of farm products to sell on the world market. This influx of subsidized commodities tends to drive down world food prices to the detriment of the poorer agricultural nations who can't compete against these artificially lowered prices. Even worse, these same nations grant their farmers export subsidies, which make their agricultural products cheaper than produce grown in developing nations.[7]

This snippet from the global food marketplace provides one illustration of the need for international cooperation to offset the inequalities created or exaggerated by domestic policies. Thus, the 1994 Agriculture Agreement of the General Agreement on Tariffs and Trade (GATT) offers some ways of ameliorating the problems of inequity caused by price supports for food produced in industrialized nations. (This international initiative is included in the Bread for the World Institute's report as a significant factor in the implementation of number 6 above.) However, there are two cautions about the political process and its ability to correct its own course.

First, policy makers need to be realistic about what can be achieved politically once a policy has created vested interests. Using the example of agricultural price supports and export subsidies, although equitable sharing would require that financial assistance somehow be restricted to small farmers who need it, and that such incentives be tied to environmentally responsible farming methods, that would be difficult to achieve politically. The policy has unwittingly generated a new constituency of big farming that now has a strong interest in maintaining the status quo. This alone explains the necessity of an international approach like GATT, which contains politically realistic provisions that gradually, rather than abruptly, reduce price supports (Finn, 140).

The second caution raises an even larger question about the prospects of political intervention in the face of inequities of economy and power. Finn observes that the possibility exists for governments of developing nations to initiate policies that favor their own rural wealthy at the expense of their rural poor. Were that to happen, it would nullify gains made through GATT's reduction of price supports. He regards this as unlikely. The move to reduce supports and improve the competitiveness of agriculture in developing nations remains the best move (Finn, 146). Nonetheless, the issue raises the specter of economic efforts at justice being compromised by unstable or undemocratic governments, or governments in the grip of powerful multinationals.

There are certainly cases that make the point. Democratically and socially minded Costa Rica, for example, has turned its agricultural export earnings into more equitable distribution of economic opportunity, resulting in substantial investment in public education and significant reductions in the proportion of chronically undernourished citizens. By contrast, Kenya's more authoritarian and less egalitarian regime has not succeeded in distributing the benefits of trade and agriculture among the population. Thus, despite the central place of agriculture in its economy, Kenya is considered by the Food and Agriculture Organization to be a "Low-Income Food Deficit Country."[8]

Local governments, local and global financial institutions, international organizations such as the United Nations and various treaty alliances, nongovernmental organizations, religious communities, and individuals must all work in concert to alleviate the great disparities of wealth and power and address the problem of hunger. Government, including every organization and citizen that participates in the shaping of government policies, has a special role to play in curbing the effects of greed and undue accumulations of wealth and power. Psalm 72:2 comes to mind:

> May he [the king] defend the cause of the
> poor of the people,
> give deliverance to the needy,
> and crush the oppressor.

Those wanting to work for change in concert with government also need to make strategic decisions about how to target their appeal. If some governments—and not only governments in developing nations—cannot be relied on to do their part in the global balancing act and international cooperation is hampered by the very inequities it seeks to dissipate, then it may be advantageous to focus attention on international business.

We have just seen that kind of attention paid to international business with a vengeance. The December 1999 meeting of the World Trade Organization, a group of delegations from member nations formed to enforce the provisions of the 1994 Uruguay Round of GATT, became a scene of sharp confrontation. Protesters took to the streets. Unions, environmentalists, and others were calling attention to child labor and unfair labor practices spurred by globalization, the compromise of environmental standards, and policies unfair to developing nations. They also demanded more participation in future WTO deliberations on the part of those who represent labor, the environment, and the marginalized.[9]

In many respect global business itself has more power to create change than government or international organizations. This is why covenants like the Caux Principles are important as a starting point for acknowledging and stimulating the social responsibility of business. A similar initiative was launched in 1989. The CERES (Coalition for Environmentally Responsible Economies) Principles commit their many business signatories to respect the limits of the environment and to be publicly accountable for doing so. To live responsibly within environmental limits, rather than hoarding, spoiling, or overconsuming resources for sheer economic gain, is to live in recognition of business's responsibility for the larger world community. Environmentally sustainable industrial growth and agricultural practice is essential to sustaining present and future generations. (It is noteworthy, given the need for many-sided efforts, that CERES is a coalition of investors, public pension trustees, foundations, labor unions, and environmental, religious, and public interest groups.)

Christians would hope, I should think, that ethical commitments like those in the Caux and CERES Principles will be the main motive for global business to become a force for greater economic justice and the alleviation of hunger and poverty. If moral suasion does not work, however, and if the intervention of government and international politics is insufficient, there is always the appeal to self-interest. Markets do not flourish and grow among people who are poor, hungry, and sick.

## GLOBAL COMMUNITY AND EUCHARISTIC COMMUNITY

In this all too brief look at this world's inequities, as refracted through the reality of hunger, the contours of global community begin to take shape. To this point, the discussion has focused on community in terms of the needs of all in contrast to the greed of some, suggesting that the priority of individual freedom, in tandem with a sense of limitlessness, needs to be tempered by concern for the welfare of the larger community. This logic was operative in identifying the need for a global ethic built on a sense of human community (and community with nature) to address disparities in the global economy. Such an understanding leads to a consideration of community in another dimension.

*Global community* can be thought of as the aggregate of human communities united by certain inescapable interdependencies and certain basic human needs and rights, which are the source of moral claims over and against the greed of special interests. But it can also be thought of in terms of international coalitions of political, economic, religious, and other organizations working toward a just response to those moral claims. The variety of coalitions and general sense of such needed cooperation mentioned in this chapter add flesh to the bones of the previous discussion of God's providential orders and the way in which they are intended to work together for the common good of creation and community.

The understanding of global community as a coalition of forces working together for the good of all will help the church locate its own mission here. It can and should make its distinct contribution to these cooperative efforts by appealing to rich traditions of God's concern for the good of all people and the wholeness of the entire creation in its advocacy for a true sense of global mutuality. Certainly the religious communities represented in the global ethic proposed by the Parliament of the World's Religions see the importance of the role of religion in the shaping of global community and see its public platform as a first step toward participation in that process. It is much the same with the international ecumenical efforts of the World Council of Churches, whose study *Christian Faith and the World Economy Today*, mentioned above, lifts up the moral necessity of placing economics within the larger framework of the divine economy in the service of the manifold values that make up the good of the human community as a whole.

In some respects, interreligious and ecumenical declarations don't have the same importance as public commitments of specific denominations. Individual denominations and their leadership are closer to the people and are far more influential in defining mission and fostering involvement. The United States Catholic Bishops' pastoral letter *Economic Justice for All* offers a book-length analysis of the United States economy and the responsibility of the church and its people to work for the poor and for justice in economic life. Despite some differences in substance and tone, other mainline denominations in America have adopted theological positions compatible with those of the Catholic bishops. Within evangelical communities, such as those associated with the Oxford conference on Christian Faith and Economics, is both a recognition of the importance of democracy and the market economy and an acknowledgment of God's demand for justice and the need to correct the injustices of present-day capitalism.[10]

As religious communities and organizations like Bread for the World look over the vast landscape of the global economy and its salient landmarks, such as hunger, a commitment to needed reforms in the name of divine justice rather than an ideological attack on capitalism grows. There is no need to demonize the market economy. There is a need to address the disparities that exist. There is a need to confront the reality of greed. And, the churches rightly sense a call to do so. More about this Christian vocation is discussed in the final chapter. For now, an observation about the global character of the church will suffice.

The church is itself a global community. In looking at the unshared goods of the global economy and reflecting on the need for an ethic based on and advanced by a global community of cooperative forces, it is important to keep this aspect of the church in mind. It is of both practical importance and theological importance.

It is of practical importance that the church is, truly, everywhere if the church's advocacy on behalf of the hungry and the poor is to be effective. The church is where people are, throughout the world. When being true to its birthright in Christ, the church is there for all people—not for its own gain—as Christ was there for all people and gave himself up on the cross for all people. Energized by the spirit of Pentecost, the church is extended geographically and culturally without limitation. Thus, the global church is potentially one of the most effective catalytic forces for an ethic of world community.

The church in its theological foundation is global as well. The church is the eucharistic community, the community whose eating and drinking of the Lord's Supper anticipates the banquet feast of the kingdom of God at which all will have a place at the table. Such eucharistic imagery works well with this discussion's theme of hunger and sharing.

In the parable of the rich man and Lazarus, the rich man feasted sumptuously and shared nothing with Lazarus, who languished in his hunger and sickness. As noted, this parable points not simply to the greedy indifference of the rich man but also to God's intention that such inequities will be reversed in the fullness of God's coming reign. Also as noted, Jesus' works of healing prefigured the ultimate victory of life and wholeness in his resurrection, and humankind's promised resurrection in the kingdom of God. The feeding of the five thousand, the only miracle recorded in all four Gospels (Matthew 14:13-21, Mark 6:32-44, Luke 9:10-17, and John 6:1-14), anticipates the eucharistic meal, instituted at the Last Supper to be the ongoing "foretaste of the feast to come." The reversal of the cruel disparities of the Lazarus parable is thus complete. In the cross and resurrection, an event of history, embodied in the sacrament of the altar, Lazarus is healed. Now, sitting at the heavenly banquet table, he will never again know hunger.

Christ emptied his very lifeblood and gave up his body to the cross so that we may never know death or hunger. "Take, eat; this is my body, given for you. . . . This is my blood of the new covenant, shed for you . . . " (Matthew 26:26-29, Luke 22:15-20, 1 Corinthians 11:23-26).

We who are the church are called the "body of Christ" (Ephesians 1:22-23), a eucharistic community that lives in hope and a community of the cross called to give itself for all.

> The cup of blessing that we bless, is it not a sharing in the blood of Christ? The bread that we break, is it not a sharing in the body of Christ? Because there is one bread, we who are many are one body, because we partake of the one bread. (1 Corinthians 10:16-17)

> Then Jesus told his disciples, "If any want to be my followers, let them deny themselves and take up their cross and follow me. Or those who want to save their life will lose it, and those who lose their life for my sake will find it. For what will it profit them if they gain the whole world but forfeit their life? (Matthew 16:24-26)

I said at the outset that advocacy on behalf of the hungry amidst the complexities of political, economic, and cultural realities in a global economy is a bit like stepping into a minefield. Once again, addressed by the word of God, there is no standing still.

## QUESTIONS FOR DISCUSSION

1.  The well-worn slogan "Think globally; act locally" is still useful encouragement. In the face of global hunger and the disparities of wealth and power it represents, what can people do locally to make a difference?
2.  Review the social statements and advocacy activities of your church body. What do they have to say about the issues of this chapter, and how can they help your congregation or church body address these issues?
3.  Review the list of "Ten Ways to Make the World Economy Work Better for Hungry People" presented by the Bread for the World Institute to help the world economy work better for hungry people. Can you think of concrete actions you can take to follow through on any of these ways?
4.  What are the ways globalization has fostered greed at the expense of those in need?

# 6
# TOWARD A SHARING SOCIETY

GIVEN THE DIRECTION OF THIS BOOK, the disposition to share and be generous is worthy of celebration as a welcome contrast to greed's incessant intrusion into human affairs. Before we become too enamored of these sibling traits, however, a word of caution from well-known pastoral theologian Henri J. M. Nouwen:

> I am increasingly convinced that one of the greatest missionary tasks is to receive the fruits of the lives of the poor, the oppressed, and the suffering as gifts offered for the salvation of the rich. We who live in the illusion of control and self-sufficiency must learn true joy, peace, forgiveness, and love from our poor brothers and sisters. As long as we only want to give, we remain in the house of fear—so much giving can be a way of staying in control.[1]

Sharing and generosity can easily become the means by which we seek to hoard power and honor and, thereby, stay in control rather than enter into community.

Sharing and generosity in the absence of a genuine and deep sense of community and sincere mutual acceptance of one another are tools for self-aggrandizement and a way to make sure that, no matter what we give, we will not give away our position of superiority. This insight is also found in several texts from the New Testament.

The first is Romans 15:26-27, where Paul is commenting on the collection taken in the churches of Macedonia and Achaia for the needy in Jerusalem. "Macedonia and Achaia have been pleased to share their resources with the poor among the saints at Jerusalem. They were pleased to do this, and indeed they owe it to them; for if the Gentiles have come to share in their spiritual blessings, they ought also be of service to them in material things."

The Greek word *koinonikos*, "to share," is from *koinonia*, "community" or "communion," sometimes translated "fellowship."

Sharing is constitutive of community, and community is constitutive of sharing. They go together. This linguistic clue is deepened by Paul's interesting remark that the churches of Macedonia and Achaia "owe it to them." They shared from a willing spirit—they were pleased to share—not simply because it was "owed," but out of a sense of mutuality. Each had something to share with the other in this exchange of material and spiritual gifts within the one communion of Christ's body.

In this picture of early church relations is a remarkable blend of obligation or responsibility toward one another and an uncoerced readiness to give generously. This is the genius of the neighbor love Christ instills and the sense of communality that goes with it: obligation does not preclude the response of love, and love does not preclude the reality of obligation. It is appropriate to the love Christ teaches. It is self-giving, in contrast to Nouwen's insight about sharing out of the need to control.

This truth is underscored when Paul says more about the spirit of the Macedonian churches' response to the appeal for the poor in Jerusalem. As a prelude to encouraging the church in Corinth to also contribute, Paul speaks of the grace enjoyed by the churches of Macedonia. "For during a severe ordeal of affliction, their abundant joy and their extreme poverty have overflowed in a wealth of generosity on their part. For I can testify, they voluntarily gave according to their means, and even beyond their means" (2 Corinthians 8:2-3).

The ability to share is itself a gift of grace from God. We love as we have first been loved; we share generously as God has shared generously with us. In noting the anticipation of God's generosity, we have a good bridge to the final text on sharing and generosity. "As for those who in the present age are rich, command them not to be haughty, or set their hopes on the uncertainty of riches, but rather on God who richly provides us with everything for our enjoyment. They are to do good, to be rich in good works, generous and ready to share, thus storing up for themselves the treasure of a good foundation for the future, so that they may take hold of life that is really life" (1 Timothy 6:17-19).

Once more, it is the spirit in which sharing and generosity are practiced that is key. There will be differences among folks as to their level of wealth, but the fact that the sufficiency of all persons is finally from God relativizes the riches of this world. Thus, the rich should not be haughty, for they are no different from anyone else. They, too, finally find their sufficiency in God who gives abundantly to all.

It is this fundamental equality in dependence upon God that forms the basis for sharing and all good works. One can hardly miss the echoes of the parable of the rich fool in Luke 12, which was discussed earlier. Wealth honestly gained is not despised, but it is meant to be shared in a spirit of genuine communality, gratitude, and love.

## POINTS OF CONTRAST AND POINTS OF CONTACT

While Christians will recognize that the ideals of generosity, sharing, and community seen in these accounts of life in the early church are a far cry from the conditions of life in the rough-and-tumble world of contemporary economic life, they will also see a connection. These ideals are God's ideals and we are God's witnesses, not only in how the community of faith comports itself as an embodiment of its message but also by how it contextualizes that message in addressing the world. These ideals speak directly to the disparities that arise out of greed. They speak to the spirit of selfish individualism that underlies greed and travels under what is the otherwise respectable banner of personal freedom. They speak to the culturally embedded tendency to excuse greed and its anticommunity impact with the belief that the unlimited nature of possibilities means there is really enough for all, if they actually want it and go after it.

Of course, all people in this vast world are not Christian, and the language of the faith will not be universally understood or respected. Yet, by speaking of God's ideal of love for neighbors and the world, points of contact emerge—points with which to connect on the path toward a sharing society amidst the out-of-whack realities of this world.

### SHARED CONTRADICTIONS AND COMMON CONCERNS

Contradictions and troubling concerns from the standpoint of faith are evident to others, who may or may not share our faith but who are troubled as well. A number of contradictions and resulting disparities in business, health care, and the global economy have already been discussed. As noted, there are people out there concerned about these matters and trying to do better. The fact that such moral insights are not the sole property of Christians does not diminish the singularity of the Christian witness; our motives are deeply rooted in the Christ and our actions point back to him. Meanwhile, the God whom we confess is the God we believe is the ruler of all and has written the divine will into the hearts of humankind, despite the perversity of our sin.

At this writing, the pot is being stirred anew at the 1999 edition of the World Economic Forum in Davos, Switzerland.[2] This gathering of more than two thousand includes an impressive array of political leaders, company chief executives, economists, bankers, investment advisors, consultants, and commentators. Much of the talk from business leaders and economists has proceeded along orthodox lines, attempting to devise policies that will reverse some of the setbacks to growth recently experienced in the emerging global economy. Yet, it has been impossible to ignore the fact that deep disparities in the wealth and well-being of nations have in many cases been exacerbated by globalization.

Egyptian president Hosni Mubarak told the forum that the global free market approach has failed the world's poor and needs to be rethought. In the developing world, he said, there is bitterness over the injustice of a system in which years of hard-won development can be virtually wiped out by changes in the market. Mubarak's dissent was joined by John J. Sweeney, head of the AFL-CIO. Sweeney claimed that the forces of globalization were exacting terrible human costs in job losses and other forms of deprivation. "Our task is not to make societies safe for globalization, but to make the global system safe for decent societies," he said.

This kind of ferment over the apparent injustices of the international economic system at a gathering like the World Economic Forum is clearly a point of contact for Christian concern and involvement. As one protest group at the forum put it, "The catastrophic result of unregulated economic growth is becoming so apparent that even the managers in their executive suites can no longer deny its results."

## HARD LESSONS

Morally bad practices do not always result in bad consequences, at least not obviously so. But there are certainly enough instances where organizations reap what they sow. These hard lessons provide a point of contact for persuasively arguing the moral alternative. This is evident in the upswing of concern for ethical business practices in the wake of a number of scandals and disasters.

Incidents like the Love Canal and the tragedy at Bhopal led the Chemical Manufacturers Association to adopt the trademarked industrywide program Responsible Care, arguably one of the most impressive commitments to public and environmental safety ever undertaken without outside regulation. In similar fashion, the Business Roundtable, in 1988, toward the end of a decade of scandal and greed, publicly committed itself to the pursuit of corporate ethics as its prime business asset.

Seemingly, there is no end of new opportunities to learn from hard lessons. Many will remember the recent debacle at Texaco. For more than a year, the corporation had been fighting a class-action lawsuit brought by African American employees who believed themselves to be victims of institutionalized prejudice at Texaco. The company's denials and efforts to fight the suit were brought to a screeching halt in a blaze of public embarrassment when tapes were released recording racial slurs by top executives and their discussion of how to destroy incriminating evidence. A costly settlement and other consequences damaging to the company ensued.[3]

The sort of entrenched bigotry that led those executives to drastic consequences has been characterized by one observer as a clear expression of an "us versus them" mentality.[4] Here, self-serving, self-protecting greed forgets the essential connectedness human beings have with one another in economic life as well as in all of life. Economic life is an integral, not separate, part of life. Competition and ambition in the absence of a clear sense of innate mutuality in human society is a sure formula for greed.

## THE HELPFUL AND THE HOPEFUL

In this discussion, I have tried not only to offer critical analysis and a realistic assessment of the difficulty of change but also a few examples of folks who are doing, or trying to do, it right. This seems like the right place to build on those examples with a reminder that there are many ways we are already a sharing society. Not everyone is always in the grip of selfish impulses like greed.

There are businesses that choose other paths to meet the exigencies of the market than simply downsizing and leaving workers and communities in the lurch. There are companies whose family-friendly provisions for employees bear witness to the recognition of a larger set of values than just the bottom line. There are industries that have gone the extra mile in environmental responsibility. There are firms who have genuinely invested in the communities where they operate. There are instances of valuable technology transfer to less-developed countries.

Conscious of the fact that sharing means giving everyone a fair chance, our society has regulated against monopoly and a variety of unfair practices. We have enacted laws to protect equal opportunity and mandate affirmative action. We have tried to make sure that all citizens have access to education, jobs, and facilities. At the national, state, and local level, we provide a wide variety of public services for people in need. These governmental initiatives are complemented by a staggering variety of charitable organizations working locally, nationally, and internationally. Church-related social ministry organizations spend billions of dollars of charitable and government funds to provide needed human services. These are joined by a significant number of world relief agencies that represent religious commitments to the alleviation of global hunger and poverty. Other church-related and secular advocacy groups lobby at state and national levels for policies that meet the needs of those underserved or not served at all.

Individuals who have amassed considerable wealth have also shown considerable philanthropy, while others of humble means continue to be examples of sacrificial giving on behalf of the needs of others. Millions of people choose careers of service rather than chasing material success as their primary goal in life. Countless caregivers literally share their lives with those in their care.

Christians will want to pray for and support these efforts. They will want to participate in the programs where possible and emulate the spirit of generosity that is evident among so many. Beyond this, we should see in these efforts at sharing, whatever their flaws may be, impulses that are points of contact for efforts to instill a spirit of sharing throughout society. The existence of these attitudes and activities is both helpful and hopeful in trying to address the underside of our culture.

Even when generous behavior is a cover for greed, such as cunning public relations on the part of a business, it is still a testimony to the fact that people admire generosity, even if they are grudgingly willing to accept greed.

We have been attempting thus far to face up to the reality of greed and to the way in which the Christian faith both exposes greed and points toward a different direction. There is still some facing up to do, but it is time to start facing instead of just facing up. We need to explore what might be done, what can be done, and what ought to be done to follow our faith and find our way toward a sharing society. We need to make the case for sharing.

## FACING OUR LIMITS

This discussion has already alluded to the limiting factor of the environment in any appraisal of the potentials of economic growth. It moves now to a somewhat more focused approach to the reality of limits in the resources of our planet and how that plays into the overall concern presented here.

The principal dialogue partner in this part of the discussion is economist Herman Daly. (Later in the chapter, some of his collaborative work with theologian John Cobb will be examined.) Daly's 1996 book, *Beyond Growth*,[5] pulls together the essential ingredients of three decades of thought. Daly is a favorite of many mainline Christian ethicists concerned with the environment, but he is far from a favorite among many mainline economists whose economics of growth he has doggedly challenged.

Daly became known in the seventies for his "steady state" economics, a perspective that evolved into what is now called "ecological economics." He is cofounder of the International Society for Ecological Economics and an associate editor of its journal, *Ecological Economics*. From 1988 to 1994, Daly was an economist with the World Bank. We cannot possibly review his economic theory here, any more than we can adequately represent other voices within the world of economics and evaluate their debates. That sort of exercise is outside the scope of this book and beyond the scope of this author's competency. What I want to do is lift up the fact that there are serious efforts to face issues of economic life that display an understanding of the need to deal with limits and confront the excesses of human aspirations for "more." Surfacing proposals like Daly's and the remarks of those who question them should serve as a catalyst in this discussion for reflections on how to move forward responsibly to our faith-based convictions.

The key to Daly's proposal is the construct that the economy is a subset of the ecosystem. Bounded by the realities of the nature's finitude, its quantitative growth cannot go on forever or it will exceed the carrying capacity of the earth with disastrous consequences of deepened inequities in the present and scarcity in the future. Consequently, Daly asserts, we need to adopt an economic policy of "sustainable development" rather than one of unlimited growth and give clear definition to the often vacuous notion of "sustainable development" (Daly, 1–23).

Sustainable development, Daly argues, requires a shift from a growth economy to a "steady state" economy (SSE), effective immediately in the North and eventually in the South. In a growth economy, there is a continual increase in the scale of matter, energy, and waste products used and produced in the economic activities of production and consumption. This process of using matter and energy and producing waste products is what Daly calls "throughput." Growth is the quantitative increase in throughput, which begins with depletion and ends in pollution. In an SSE, the total throughput is constant, although its allocation may change as the market changes. "Qualitative improvement in the use made of given scale of throughput, resulting either from improved technical knowledge or from a deeper understanding of purpose, is called 'development.' An SSE therefore can develop, but cannot grow, just as the planet earth of which it is a subsystem can develop without growing" (Daly, 31).

An SSE respects two limits that a growth economy chooses to ignore. The first is the biophysical limits of growth. These limits are a product of three interrelated conditions: (1) the finitude of the planet's resources, (2) the reality of entropy (the second law of thermodynamics) that prevents our ability to be totally efficient and totally able to recycle, and (3) ecological interdependence, meaning impact on one part of the ecosystem will reverberate to other parts. The unwillingness of growth economists to accept these limits as placing limits on economic growth Daly believes flies in the face of the obvious. Nonetheless, growth economists cling to the limitless growth scenario because they attribute to humanity a limitless ingenuity for harnessing nature's finite resources (Daly, 33–35).

The second set of limits, which Daly calls "ethicosocial," involves four propositions that, in one way or another, express three principles of environmental justice: sustainability, sufficiency, and solidarity. *Sustainability* refers to the ecosystems of the planet being able to sustain themselves. In this regard, Daly's propositions involve concern for future generations and the survival of sentient subhuman species. *Sufficiency,* as the term suggests, means a level of sustainability in which all have sufficient resources for their own well-being, including their survival. Sufficiency also implies a level of affluence that is "enough," rather than an approach to wealth that is devoted to "more." *Solidarity* is a moral commitment to stand together with, and act on behalf of, those whose well-being is being threatened or undermined, both now or in the future. Sufficiency and solidarity lurk in Daly's four propositions, which question growth's ability to positively affect well-being and happiness. His fourth proposition is worth quoting in part:

> *The desirability of aggregate growth is limited by the corrosive effects on moral standards resulting from the very attitudes that foster growth, such as the glorification of self-interest and a scientific-technocratic worldview.* On the demand side of commodity markets, growth is stimulated by greed and acquisitiveness, intensified beyond the "natural" endowment from original sin by the multibillion-dollar advertising industry. On the supply side, technocratic scientism proclaims the possibility of limitless expansion and preaches a reductionistic, mechanistic philosophy, which, in spite of its success as a research program, has serious shortcomings as a worldview. (Daly, 37)

There are, as has been suggested, other perspectives than the sort Daly offers. One can infer from his debate with the proponents of growth what the broad outlines of the antithetical position would be. There is also, however, a different slant on things from among those whose values are more congenial to Daly's.

Mark Sagoff, in his June 1997 article in *The Atlantic Monthly* entitled "Do We Consume Too Much?"[6] assesses these matters in a somewhat different and quite interesting manner. He begins by observing that arguments over the future of the planet tend to be dominated by those who claim that the expanding economy will use up the earth's resources and those who see no reason whatsoever to limit growth. As far as Sagoff is concerned, they both have it wrong (Sagoff, 1–3).

The bulk of the article is devoted to debunking the conviction that increasing consumption will inevitably lead to depletion and scarcity. As plausible as this position may seem, he believes it to be mistaken both in principle and in fact. Sagoff claims it is based on four misconceptions. The first three: (1) that we are running out of raw materials; (2) that we are running out of food and timber; and (3) that we are running out of energy. In each case, he offers an elaborate argument as to why ingenuity has already enabled realistic steps to deal with these issues, and why ingenuity will enable effective steps in the future. Based on a population projected by some experts to level off at 10 billion during the coming century, Sagoff believes sustainable growth and the ability to make necessary technical changes to control the problems of pollution are possible. Moreover, with the transfer of needed, environmentally friendly technologies to developing nations, they too can be players in the expanding global economy (Sagoff, 3–11).

Although related, Sagoff's fourth misconception is of a somewhat different order. The idea that the North exploits the South, using up its resources in overconsumption, is faulty. As leaders in the South will often say, the real problem is that the North doesn't buy enough of what the South produces. The problem isn't the level of consumption, but whose stuff is consumed. If free trade is allowed in agricultural products, for example, the South could sell the North a good deal more. According to Sagoff, we need to maximize the export of products appropriate to our soils and let nations of the South sell us commodities appropriate to their soils. This would be friendly to the environment and to the global economic order. Instead, as was seen in the previous discussion of Finn's analysis of free trade, we protect agriculture to the detriment of our own poor, who pay for that protection in higher food costs, and to the detriment of poor countries who can't compete. Also, we subsidize the start-up of agricultural industries on our own soil that are already well established, and are ecologically and economically less expensive, in the South (Sagoff, 12–15).

Sagoff recognizes that the possibilities for sustainable growth are in large measure subject to the vicissitudes of governmental will and corruption. The moral and democratic infrastructure, he says, is the key to creating this better world for everyone. In fact, it is the moral argument regarding consumption that he wants to make. If ecological doomsayers can be challenged by exposing their misconceptions, then the proponents of limitless growth can be challenged for promoting materialism.

The problem with unbridled consumption is not what it is doing or will do to the sustainability of the environment, but what it is doing to us. It creates the extreme imbalances of wealth already noted. It erodes community and relativizes values under the pressure of our drive for economic gain. We destroy ourselves to work harder for things that don't make us happier. Nature becomes but a resource instead of a source of wonder and beauty. It is the "commodification" of life that was noted in chapter 1. Reflecting on an article in Daly's own journal, *Ecological Economics*, by economist Robert H. Nelson, Sagoff concludes, "As long as the debate over sustainability is framed in terms of the physical limits of growth rather than the moral purpose of it, mainstream economic theory will have the better argument" (Sagoff, 17–20). Daly, in turn, believes that Sagoff fails to pay adequate attention to the consequences of our actions. A prudential consideration of the costs and benefits of our patterns of consumption is part of our moral calculus as well as discerning our inherent duties.[7]

Whatever their differences in scientific and economic analysis of the world situation, both Daly and Sagoff recognize that, whatever environmental limits must be faced, facing what Daly calls the ethicosocial limits is essential. No doubt this is why Daly, in his own writings and in his collaboration with John Cobb, finally appeals to a theologically grounded moral argument.

## FACING ONE ANOTHER

In facing one another, we set the issue of community over prevailing sentiments of individualism. John Cobb and Herman Daly make the emphasis on community a key starting point for what they propose in their lucidly titled and widely read book *For the Common Good: Redirecting the Economy toward Community, the Environment, and a Sustainable Future*.[8] Economic historian Karl Polanyi's insight that in a capitalist society social relations are embedded in the economic system instead of the reverse is a starting point for Daly and Cobb. It is this state of affairs that needs to be changed. The economy should be a servant of community rather than the community being dissipated by economic forces. As with Daly's notion that the economy is a subset of the ecology, so the market is a subset of society (Daly and Cobb, 8–15).

Practicing sustainable development and working toward the elimination of the world's gross inequalities is working for the common good, for the interests of the entire human community, rather than working simply for the freedom and prerogatives of the individual or of individual groups. (This is not a plea for socialism, veiled or otherwise, however. Daly and Cobb clearly believe in private ownership.)

Seeing the economy as a servant of community means seeing economic forces and institutions in the context of a larger complex of values. This is the economics of *oikonomia,* meaning "household." The economics of *oikonomia* is the economics of community, which looks at economic activity in relation to all values integral to human community, including cultural, spiritual, institutional, historical, biological, and land. In this view, economic activity is not narrowly understood as simply the process and dynamic of monetary exchange. It is integrated with the study of the humanities. Academic circles separate these fields into isolated specialties. "In reality political, social, economic, and cultural aspects of human existence are indissolubly interconnected" (Daly and Cobb, 127, 138–45).

The economics of community must not only be developed in an interdisciplinary dialogue, its progress must be measured by a more comprehensive index than the GNP. The GNP, Daly and Cobb observe, is only a measure of economic activity; it is narrowly quantitative. Increase in GNP does not necessarily mean increase in economic welfare. That is, simple growth is not always simply good. It does not reveal how quality of life is faring under prevailing economic conditions. Instead, Daly and Cobb have developed a remarkable Index of Sustainable Economic Welfare, which records and correlates a number of factors, including equality of income distribution; improvement in health, education, and public services; costs of pollution; loss of resources; and so on (Daly and Cobb, 443ff.). A one-dimensional measurement such as GNP can easily mask the fact that things are still very much out of whack and, when the numbers look good, provide a cover of justification for those who profit most.

Daly's and Cobb's insistence on seeing economic life in the larger context of many values seems a clear corollary to the kind of collaborative activities mentioned in the previous chapter. As was suggested, cooperation between multiple constituencies, representing different interests, is needed to effectively confront the inequities of the global economy and move in the direction of a greater sense of global community.

For Daly and Cobb, however, the concern for community is more sharply drawn than supporting collaborative efforts to look out for the interests of all. For them, the common good is served when economic activity is controlled locally, in communities and for communities. For this reason, they object to free trade as currently practiced. Private, multinational economic interests without loyalties to any national communities move capital as well as goods across national boundaries whenever it is financially advantageous to do so, resulting in sudden and damaging blows to local economies and the communities founded on them. This, they say, is the triumph of individualism over community. Ideally, there should be trade between nations as communities. Such trade enables each nation to preserve and develop its own particular industries and preserve local economic stability through the regulation of capital outflow (Daly and Cobb, 209–35).

It is not difficult to find conscientious Christians who share similar concerns but who would oppose certain of Daly's and Cobb's proposals. A cautious and realistic endorsement of free trade has already been seen in the Bread for the World Institute Report. Moreover, it is not only the case that controversial trade policy proposals are debatable among people of goodwill. As Michael Novak has pointed out, what constitutes the common goodwill always be open to debate when one of the goods included is the freedom of individuals. A diversity of views and priorities is inevitable.[9] Thus, even the Index of Sustainable Economic Welfare, while certainly preferable to the GNP as a measure of the common good, will not be able to satisfy everyone.

In the final analysis, as we face one another and attempt in good faith to share with one another for the common good, there is a certain commonsense recognition of what is needed, even as we struggle with competing scenarios. There is also a sense of what is simply not adequate. Despite a significantly different outlook from that of Daly and Cobb, Michael Novak is able to cite this classic principle of Catholic thought with approval: "To argue that the private pursuit of wealth results in the best outcome for the entire society is to view the common good as 'merely an unintended accidental consequence.' This falls short of the Catholic concept of the common good."[10] However we define it, we need to intend it and seek it for one another. One step in that direction, as it concerns economic life, is to turn aside from the prevailing notion that a market economy is driven only by self-interested competitiveness. In the next chapter, we shall look at one instance of how that may work out in actual practice.

## FACING OUR LIMITATIONS

We have spoken repeatedly now of limitations, the undeniable reality of human sin that refuses to recognize its limits: the limits inherent in our dependent relationship with God, the limits of the resources of our world, and the limits imposed by the need to consider the well-being of our neighbors in the various communities that comprise human existence. In greed's drive to produce, spend, and acquire, it proceeds under the banner of individual freedom and limitless possibilities, manifesting itself in unbridled competitiveness. By contrast, we have been exploring the need for a more community-minded approach of cooperation among various entities in the service of a more sharing society and a more equitable global and local community.

Competition versus cooperation—that is a key issue. So said the World Council of Churches study on the world economy. It is a question of what shall motivate us in approaching economic policy as we attempt to balance individual freedoms and communal and natural necessities. It is a question we must face in facing our limitations.

> Those who trust in the market are relying on competition, and will readily regard others as naive for expecting co-operation to work in a sinful world. Those who have had encouraging experiences of co-operation will insist that competition is bound to prove harmful if it is allowed more than a limited place. In part this is a theological debate, between those who trust in the "already" of the salvation offered in Christ and want to work it out in the practice of co-operation, and those who believe that the achievement of salvation is "yet to come" and that meanwhile human behavior must take the fallen-ness of humanity fully into account.[11]

As the World Council Study recognizes, both views have a point.

Christians are both realists and idealists at one and the same time. We live neither in the "already" nor in the "not yet." We live in the tension of both. God's future kingdom of salvation for our world has broken into our present as a certain promise in the victory of the Christ over sin and death. That future has not yet arrived in its fullness, however. We cannot ignore the lingering and profound reality of sin that still pervades our world, even as that sin awaits its inevitable demise in the arrival of God's future. At the same time, we cannot ignore the power of God's creating spirit to work change and transformation, and we cannot ignore our call to ride on the wings of the spirit in working toward those promised values of God's coming kingdom. These "kingdom" values of life, wholeness, peace, equality, freedom, and community provide Christians with a compass that guides them in their quest to promote the common good.

Practically speaking, the tension between "already" and "not yet" means both competition and cooperation. Competition engaged in honesty and couched in cooperative measures that help to curb greed and serve the larger good is an arrangement that can help balance individual freedom and responsibility for the neighbor. Competition is not inherently the sign of fallen existence, and cooperation is not necessarily the evidence of redemption. In that sense, the World Council's analysis is off the mark. Both competition and cooperation can be channeled toward self-interest or serving one another. Both can, in their own ways, work against selfish tendencies.

In advancing the agenda of the Christian ethic to offset greed in individual practices or in social, political, and economic arrangements, the key is to work toward the values of the kingdom through those measures that most closely approximate the other-directedness of the neighbor love Jesus commanded. This is the spiritual-ethical leaven of the Christian contribution to a sharing society.

## I DESIRE MERCY, NOT SACRIFICE

At the 1998 international meeting of Anglican bishops at Lambeth, the bishops challenged governments and international financial institutions to face up to the need of forgiving the debts of developing nations in an effort to enable poor countries to move forward toward a more acceptable standard of living and economic development. This call is paralleled by the Jubilee 2000 campaign being promoted by a broad coalition of religious and environmental groups, with the support of the pope and the archbishop of Canterbury. The campaign takes its theme from the jubilee tradition recorded in Leviticus 25. According to this account, God commanded that every fiftieth year a jubilee be declared. In the jubilee year, debts are forgiven and families are reunited on their lands.

Not surprisingly, the declaration at Lambeth and the idea of

92    GREED

the jubilee year has aroused some criticism from those who believe that such appeals are overly simplistic in the face of hard economic and political realities and, consequently, are little more than pious sentiment.

From the standpoint of the Bible, however, the jubilee year is an indication of the pervasive message that God's justice begins with mercy. There will be a need to devise principles, pursue strategies, and engage in careful analysis in confronting the issues of economic justice and injustice that lie behind Lambeth and the Jubilee 2000 campaign. As far as the Bible is concerned, however, the first question to ask is one of mercy: Of those in need, whom do we need to help? The strategy for the "how" follows after the commitment of mercy has already been made.

This is basically the challenge of Jesus' confrontation with the Pharisees when he said to them, "Go and learn what this means, I desire mercy, not sacrifice." The strict adherence to religious codes and practices that characterized pharisaic piety represented a shallow righteousness in the absence of mercy and compassion for the neighbor.

Adherence to strict economic policies and legal precedents or political calculations when these considerations are not motivated by mercy and designed to serve those in need are not defensible under the canons of God's justice. Mercy is the clear link between love and justice in the Christian ethos. As 1 John 3:17 puts it simply and powerfully in this rhetorical question, "How does God's love abide in anyone who has the world's goods and sees a brother or sister in need and yet refuses help?"

All are not Christians, of course. All are not driven by Christlike love. The realities of life in a fallen and ambiguous world are likely to be fragmentary and riddled with compromise. Nonetheless, "the mediocre realities of our present . . . are to be nurtured for the intuitions of the ultimate they possess."[12] Therefore, the Christian agenda is to strive toward those values of God's promised reign through measures that most closely approximate the other-directedness of Christian neighbor love.

The challenge of the jubilee year and contemporary proposals for its revival recall the unconditional character of God's love and the unconditional character of the love we in return are called to show by considering a forgiveness of financial debt that, for all its magnitude, is but a small replica of the enormous debt of sin God has for-given. One is put in mind of the parable of the unforgiving servant who, having been forgiven a staggering debt, immediately went out and had a fellow servant thrown in prison because he could not repay the pittance he owed him (Matthew 18:23-30). Some of the pettiness of human behavior is reflected in the unforgiving servant; it is the pettiness of judgment. Yet, the parable's final word is that God, like the king who forgave his servant's huge debt, is unlimited in mercy and forgiveness. We draw strength from our faith in that promise of working toward a sharing society.

In the meantime, God's gracious and creative hand makes itself felt in myriad and remarkable ways. We have seen that a combina-tion of government regulation and industry initiatives has begun to move us toward a more environmentally sustainable approach to development, an approach that will help protect the possibility of sufficiency in a more equitable world. We have noted other evidences of our sharing society. Even the staggering challenge of debt relief is not without precedent in history,[13] and there are good practical rea-sons why it can be a reasonable course of action once again.

## I DESIRE FREEDOM, NOT FEAR

Jesus might well have said something like this himself. Mercy is an act of freedom, while "sacrifice" easily becomes an act of fear, an effort to placate God and escape punishment.

Here, we revisit Luther's thoughts on Christian freedom, men-tioned briefly at the end of chapter 4. The freedom from concern for our own fate that comes with knowing we are unconditionally accepted by God enables us to serve our neighbor in love. If it is true that personal freedom in our culture has often been used to prop up individualistic values at the expense of community values, the notion of Christian freedom is quite different. For Christians, sharing is a sign of freedom. It is a freedom from fear for our own well-being that enables us to risk being open to the needs of our neighbor. Again, Jesus is our prototype of perfect freedom, as Paul tells us in Philippians 2:4ff.: "Let each of you look not to your own interests, but to the interests of others. Let the same mind be in you that was in Christ Jesus, who, though he was in the form of God, did not count equality with God something to be exploited, but emptied himself."

Being served and accepted by God's universal love begets equality for all and freedom to serve. Freedom to serve begets equality among all through loving service. And being affirmed and accepted by God and each other sets us free to serve. The cycle begins anew. To celebrate the freedom of the individual without regard to equality often leaves those who suffer the negative effects of inequality without the resources or the opportunities to exercise their freedom in meaningful ways. We cannot claim to extend freedom to all if we do not attend to the needs of all.

One brief illustration helps to make the point. In the Americans with Disabilities Act are legal requirements to provide reasonable accommodations for persons with disabilities so that they are truly free to participate in the opportunities of work and society. We recognize in this sort of legislative action that personal freedom and equal opportunity are hollow notions if people are prevented from exercising them. To the extent that the inequalities of economic and political life severely limit real choice and opportunity for countless numbers, freedom is not actually the right of everyone; in reality, it is only the privilege of the powerful.

## QUESTIONS FOR DISCUSSION

1. Review chapter 2. What themes in that chapter connect with points made in this chapter?
2. Can you think of ways we share as a society beyond those mentioned in this chapter?
3. We have spoken of the difficulty of finding consensus over what constitutes the "common good." What features of this elusive common good do you see as obvious? How are they related to the values promised in God's future reign?
4. Can you think of ways in which competition serves the larger community?

# 7
# STAKEHOLDER CAPITALISM:
# A CASE STUDY IN SHARING

> Every individual . . . neither intends to promote the public interest, nor knows how much he is promoting it. . . . By directing [his] industry in such a manner as its produce may be of greatest value, he intends only his own gain, and he is in this, as in many other cases, led by an invisible hand to promote an end which was no part of his intention. Nor is it always the worse for society that it was no part of it. By pursuing his own interest he frequently promotes that of society more effectually than when he really intends to promote it. I have never known much good done by those who affected to trade for the public good.[1]

This quotation from Adam Smith's *Wealth of Nations* is perhaps one of the most familiar and oft cited from that landmark study of the eighteenth century. It is a "proof text" for those who defend laissez-faire capitalism and contend that we are all better off if the markets are allowed to proceed virtually unencumbered by government interference. It is also the text that has won for Adam Smith the reputation of being the "high priest of selfishness, greed, and materialism."[2]

Adam Smith's theory has been revisited by a number of scholars in recent times. These thinkers have come to the conclusion that he can neither be blamed for selfishness and greed as a modus operandi for business nor be invoked in support of a completely unfettered capitalism. On the contrary, scholars contend, Smith placed a high premium on an established system of justice based on fairness and he clearly recognized the need for social policies that would channel self-interest in the service of public good. Nowhere in *Wealth of Nations* does Smith praise avarice or the unbridled pursuit of personal advantage.[3]

Over and against the amoral theory of business, which is often attributed to the enormous influence of Adam Smith's work, is a portrait of Smith as keenly aware of the need for a moral infrastructure within which free enterprise must function if it is to serve the common good. Serving the common good was in fact Smith's aim, through a system of wealth creation. All along, it seems, he was banking on an established context of culturally embedded morality to give moral compass to the workings of the "unseen hand."[4]

The rehabilitation of Adam Smith is part of a movement, which has gained considerable momentum during the past two decades, calling for greater attention to the ethical conduct and social responsibility of the business enterprise. One prominent manifestation of these concerns is the emergence of stakeholder theory or stakeholder capitalism, the focus of this chapter. Stakeholder theory offers a case study in sharing. First, though, a preliminary look at the ethical challenge is useful, both in terms of some of the considerations that prompt stakeholder thinking and some of the ethical foundations on which it might rest.

## THE ETHICAL CHALLENGE

Some of the concerns that lie behind the urging of a stakeholder approach to business have already been discussed. Chapter 3, for example, showed the terrible impact downsizing has had on individuals, communities, and others. While these folks were suffering the fallout of downsizing, stockholders were enjoying a nice increase in share values. A good dose of downsizing seems to be a quick way to boost sagging numbers and consolidate good relations between top management and shareholders. Moreover, the prevailing assumption that stockholders are the owners of the company and their profit is the company's purpose appears to be grounds enough for many leaders in business to embrace this practice.

By contrast, in God's providential plan, the economic order is but one of a number of orders in human society, all of which are interrelated for the purpose of serving the general well-being. Economic order does not travel in a separate orbit. When its activities detract from the commonweal, it may well need to be adjusted, as through government regulation, for example. The concentration of wealth and power in the hands of the one group—stockholders and top management—at the expense of employees, communities, and others affiliated with the business is not only a disordered state of affairs, it also fails the test of sharing at the core of the biblical ethic of Christian neighbor love.

In a manner not unlike this orientation of the Christian tradition, sociologist and communitarian Amitai Etzioni has argued that the market cannot ignore its social embeddedness. It cannot pretend to operate in isolation from the interests and needs of the rest of society. In the communitarian perspective, both the individual and the community matter, and they live together in a web of mutual obligations. Thus, for example, individual property rights are certainly to be respected, but they carry with them certain responsibilities to others. Consequently, in the case of individual financial organizations, their justification resides in their contribution to the larger community, not simply in the profit delivered to shareholders.[5]

Arguing from an ethic of duty, moral philosopher Robert Solomon has insisted that business has responsibilities to its surrounding community. The ethical obligations held toward one another are a function of the fact that community is constitutive of human existence. Solomon takes an Aristotelian view that life is an organic unity in which individual interests and the interests of the community are inseparable. Given those morally charged presuppositions, the purpose of business is to serve people, not just to make a profit.[6] For Etzioni, the communitarian, and Solomon, the philosopher of duty, the move to stakeholder thinking is logical and obvious.

For another commentator, the ethical obligations implied in stakeholder capitalism are based on the simple fact that most of life, including the health and safety of employees and customers, the livelihoods of individuals and communities, issues of social justice such as racism and sexism, and the integrity of the emerging global financial order, are heavily influenced by what corporations do or do not do.[7] It is a basic principle of justice that those who are affected by the policies or actions of a group should be able in some way to participate or be represented in the process that impinges on their lives.

How this participation works in democratic societies seems clear, even if it is imperfect. We the people are represented in government. We have opportunities for public hearings on matters of policy and, in some cases, can vote directly by referendum. Lobbyists press government on behalf of myriad causes and groups. It appears, however, that we are less surefooted when it comes to consistently applying the principles of representation and participation to stakeholder theory.

It is perhaps complicated even further when we consider that advocates of stakeholder theory would now want to add the environment to the list of those having a stake in the actions of corporations. For someone like Herman Daly, the environment is certainly a definitive stakeholder. But who speaks the definitive word for the environment? How do we adjudicate among the needs and aspirations of stakeholders in a global economy, especially when the movement of capital enables companies to buy cheap labor anywhere, raising the standard for those laborers but damaging the prospects of stakeholders in the labor force back home?

A definition of *stakeholder theory* may be helpful at this point.

## MORE ABOUT STAKEHOLDER THEORY AND ANALYSIS

To begin, *stakeholder theory,* or *stakeholder capitalism,* can be distinguished from *stakeholder analysis.* The former is the proposal or conviction, usually based on both pragmatic and moral grounds, that businesses can and ought to consider the interests of all individuals and groups who have a stake in the activities of the company. *Stakeholder analysis* is the process of identifying stakeholders and determining how to respond to their varied needs and interests.

Philosopher and business ethicist Richard De George believes that inherent in stakeholder capitalism is a moral obligation based on the premise that corporations have responsibilities to many constituencies. Given the nature of those responsibilities, such as the safety of workers, consumers, and the environment, it is not at all clear that the interests of shareholders—who are among the stakeholders—should always take precedence. Having arrived at this conclusion, De George defines *stakeholder analysis* as "weighing and balancing all of the competing moral demands on a firm by each of those who have a claim on it, in order to arrive at the firm's moral obligation in any particular case."[8] In stakeholder analysis, profitability is not the only consideration in management decision making.

Stakeholders not only have moral claims on behalf of their needs and interests, they also exert a certain amount of influence on a company's strategic planning. Heidi Vernon has distinguished between those stakeholders, internal and external to the firm, who have direct influence and those who have indirect influence. External stakeholders with direct influence include suppliers, customers, competitors, and government. External stakeholders with indirect influence include social activist groups, religious institutions, regulators, local community, media, trade associations, lobbies, and political action committees. Internal stakeholders with direct influence are boards of directors and employees. Unions and shareholders are, then, internal stakeholders with indirect influence.[9]

Vernon goes on to present the variety of ways management tactics already in place represent a concerted effort to respond to stakeholder influence. For example, customer service departments, marketing research, and customer product testing are obvious and long-standing ways to keep communication flowing and maximize satisfaction. Most obvious is the need to provide safe, high-quality products and services at a fair price. In dealing with communities, businesses often have community relations offices, seek to buy and employ locally whenever possible, support local charities, engage in joint education programs, and sometimes get involved in urban renewal projects. With regard to activist groups, among other things, companies can try to internalize their concerns in company policy making, consult with them on sensitive matters, and even offer representation on their board of directors.[10]

That business is enmeshed in the societies where it operates is clear. That it must be responsive to various groups within those societies that believe they have a stake in the conduct of that business is also clear. That management has adopted a variety of tactics for responding is evident. Nevertheless, the question remains as to what extent management is simply trying manage stakeholder influences or feels it has a genuine moral obligation to these individuals and groups, as Solomon, Etzioni, De George, and many others would have it. Chances are, it ends up being both in practice, even in the most enlightened organizations. But our concern here is that firms start from the premise that there is an obligation to stakeholders and that strategic planning and ongoing decisions follow from that. We are looking for a corporate culture committed to sharing fairly in the community of relationships with which it is involved.

## ETHICAL PERSPECTIVES ON STAKEHOLDER CAPITALISM

Some ethical dimensions of stakeholder theory have already been alluded to. Certainly the Christian ethic of sharing points in the direction of stakeholder thinking. Now we look at a few examples of ethically sensitive discussions of stakeholder capitalism from within the discourse of business ethics.

## MOVING BEYOND SOCIAL RESPONSIBILITY

Much of the talk about stakeholder capitalism has its origins in debates over corporate social responsibility. Although debate over the concept of corporate social responsibility has been widespread, it was in fact resolved by the pressure of various stakeholders during the sixties and seventies. Consumer groups, political groups, and religious groups all brought pressure on business to be responsive to a variety of stakeholders. The crusade of Ralph Nader, boycotts and stockholder petitions by religious groups in protest of marketing infant formula in developing nations, or doing business in South Africa—these are examples of the types of activities that helped to make social responsiveness an accepted part of management practice.

Despite the logic of moving from social responsibility to stakeholder theory, however, two of the more influential spokespersons for stakeholder theory have suggested reconsidering that connection. Business ethicists R. Edward Freeman and Jeanne Liedka have argued that corporate social responsibility is an outmoded idea. It perpetuates old assumptions about business as an enterprise distinct from the rest of society with its own rules and logic. While business has some responsibilities to society, business and society are separable. Freeman and Liedka say that corporations should be thought of, not as having a responsibility to society, but as being an integral part of society in a web of relationships and values. Corporations are networks of stakeholder interest in which individuals and groups engage in caring activities aimed at mutual support and achievement. Theirs is an ethos of caring and community: corporations are a means through which "to pursue the joint ends of individual and collective good."[11]

This type of approach is also reflected in what business ethicist Laura Nash has described as a "covenantal business ethic." The covenantal ethic takes as the purpose of business the creation of value and establishing mutually beneficial relationships. "A Covenantal Ethic does not just respect other people's needs, it takes them to be the *first* purpose of business thinking. In so doing the Covenantal Ethic prompts a different set of psychological attitudes or character traits than do the self-interest assumptions."[12]

In a more recent piece, Freeman relates stakeholder capitalism and the problem of poverty in a capitalist society. He takes his cue from the position of Cornel West, a prominent thinker and social analyst: to overcome the hopelessness that breeds poverty, we need a politic that offers hope that we can struggle together for a meaningful life; within a prophetic framework, a guiding moral vision. West allows no role for capitalism, while Freeman believes that retelling the story of capitalism in a particular way can contribute to that needed prophetic framework, and thus to a new way of doing things that can help generate hope in the fight against poverty.[13]

This new story of capitalism is that of stakeholder capitalism, in which corporations are places where all stakeholders pursue their joint interests. Freeman speaks of groups such as suppliers, customers, employees, financiers, and communities. "One thrives when all thrive, and when the interests of one group are systematically discounted over time, all suffer. . . . Directors of corporations have a duty of care to stakeholders, and managers are agents of multiple principals" (Freeman, 33).

The sense of mutual struggle in the bonds of care, it seems, provides Freeman with a business version of West's political-prophetic vision. And, Freeman sees it happening. He offers a number of examples of corporations in which stakeholder orientation has taken hold.

At Johnsonville Sausage, based in Wisconsin, employees do the hiring and firing. They work in teams to set production schedules, engage in planning, and do quality control. Workers relate directly to consumers to deal with problems. They share in the profits, and their salaries are tied to their improving skills and knowledge in classes provided by the company. There are job coaches, but no supervisors.

At Motorola, a global leader in cellular phones and other high-tech products, there are no layoffs. Employees attend a corporate university for two or three weeks each year. When an individual worker's skills become obsolete, they are offered retraining. There is a sense of strong togetherness in a mutual commitment to quality that serves all of the company's constituents well. The emphasis on quality began when a manager got up at a large meeting and criticized the company's products. "Rather than being executed, this manager became a hero" (Freeman, 33).

No doubt there are warts to be found on these firms, and there may be some companies that use their ethical vision as a marketing tool. There may even be very few operations in which stakeholder capitalism is fully integrated into company policy and practice. Nonetheless, it is important that tangible progress is being made by big and small organizations alike, even if the motives are sometimes mixed and the results are sometimes incomplete.

It is also important that stakeholder theory is being worked on in both small and large businesses, for each has an impact on communal life and each has distinct opportunities and problems. A small business may find it easier in some ways to build a sense of teamwork and investment in the business and its community. But a small business's resources may well be too limited to sustain its relationships when serious economic shifts occur. Large, publicly traded corporations may well have the resources to sustain a stakeholder approach to management even in times of economic downturn. But they have the difficulty of managing their size and dealing with the pressures of stockholders and global competition. Both can learn from each other and both can support each other.

To morally significant notions like community, cooperation, covenant, and caring, which embody a spirit quite different from the kind of individualism that underlies greed, we now add the principle of "fairness." In a recent *Business Ethics Quarterly* article, Robert A. Phillips proposes the principle of fairness be used both to give moral weight to a firm's obligations to stakeholders and to help identify who the legitimate stakeholders are. Simply told, the principle of fairness dictates that special obligations of responsibility are owed to the interests of those who are "voluntary members of a cooperative scheme for mutual benefit." This, in turn, defines who the stakeholders are, that is, voluntary members of a cooperative scheme for mutual benefit.[14]

A paradigm shift is lurking here, a shift in which business transactions are seen more in terms of cooperative schemes than in terms of cutthroat competition. If stakeholders are seen as partners in a mutually beneficial venture, they become less the source of conflicts or individuals and groups whose aspirations need to be managed.[15]

To the extent that Phillips's model helps to identify who the stakeholders are, it makes an important contribution to making stakeholder management manageable. At the same time, such a definition would seem to exclude the environment, which Robert Solomon has called "the silent stakeholder." It may even exclude groups that attempt to speak for the environment. Virtually everyone recognizes that nature cannot be left out of the equation. Its health and sustainability are too important to all stakeholders, now and in the future, not to mention out of respect for its own integrity. To Phillips's credit, he points out that the special obligations owed to stakeholders are over and above basic moral obligations individuals and firms owe to all elements of society. Perhaps this covers the environment, but one suspects there is more conceptual work to be done at this point.

## A NEW LOOK AT OWNERSHIP

The fairness-based model attempts to link moral obligations to stakeholders to the conditions of stakeholder membership in an interdependent, even circular, fashion. The nature of the relationship that constitutes stakeholder status is what invokes and gives concreteness to the principle of fairness. In fact, the type of relationship in which fairness is invoked defines what a stakeholder is.

The important and interesting work of Margaret Blair explains how establishing stakeholder membership becomes the basis of management's obligations to them. Margaret Blair is a senior fellow at the Brookings Institution in Washington, D.C., and has also been a correspondent and bureau chief for *Business Week*. Fundamental to her argument that corporations have a larger obligation, to a greater number of claimants, than simply the obligation to maximize return for shareholders is her challenge to traditional assumptions about "ownership" in corporate reality. The idea that shareholders are the owners leads to certain conclusions about corporate governance that focuses benefits on shareholders to the exclusion of rightful claims by others who should also be recognized as stakeholders. Blair does not believe that concept is tenable. Ownership has been parceled out to a variety of participants in the corporate enterprise. Rethinking the meaning of ownership in light of present realities leads to a better determination of who the stakeholders are.[16]

At issue in defining ownership is the question of control. If shareholders are the owners, it is argued, they should have the right to control and should be expected to exercise that control to their own benefit. The corollary notion that it is management's purpose to increase profits for shareholders, then, leads to such actions as downsizing and closing operations that, although financially viable, are not maximally profitable for stockholders.[17] In a publicly traded corporation, however, the rights of property ownership are diffused. Stockholders get the right to some return and a very limited right of control. Actual possession, use, and control of the property reside with the managers. Moreover, the rights of property ownership are generally understood to be based on some socially constructed idea of distributive justice that determines who has a moral claim on assets. Under distributive justice, those having claims will include not only those who hold stock but also those who have put certain efforts into the company, made certain sacrifices, have certain needs, and so on.[18]

If the meaning of ownership is reconsidered in light of what corporations really look like and the principles of justice that underlie property rights, it becomes clear that a number of stakeholders other than stockholders share in ownership and the considerations that accrue. For Blair, this ownership-stakeholder status belongs to those who have "substantial firm-specific investments at risk." This includes shareholders, but it can conceivably include suppliers who have made significant commitments involving risks, communities that have invested in the firm through certain public accommodations, and employees who have made firm-specific career commitments.[19] As an example of Blair's proposal, let's look at the last group.

Employees who represent firm-specific human capital built up over time are investing and risking themselves in ways analogous to the way investors risk their money. Firm-specific skills are often technical skills associated with the particularities of a given firm's production. Such skills may also be in the form of specific knowledge or networks of personal relationships valuable or essential to the company business. They are a genuine risk investment in the firm because they are likely not to be nearly as useful or valuable in another employment situation. These skills are human capital, capital in the real sense that they are basic to the creation of wealth by the corporation. Given this analysis, Blair maintains that such employees should be treated as stakeholders along with shareholders. For example, she suggests that employees be compensated with shares in the equity of the corporation for their firm-specific skills, while being paid a fair wage for those skills that are generic and portable from one employment situation to another.[20]

Having recast some basic assumptions about ownership and stakeholder status, Blair offers a corollary principle regarding the purpose of corporations and their governance. Corporations exist to create wealth for the whole of society. Their governance should be designed to meet that goal. This entails taking all stakeholders into account in corporate decision making. At any given time or in any given circumstance, some stakeholders will command more attention than others, but all remain as part of the equation. In cases of employees with firm-specific skills, the relationship should be formalized through stock compensation and voting privileges. Blair realizes that on various features of her proposal, the law is either silent or would need to be changed.[21]

Blair has tried to integrate an ethical concern for the sharing of wealth into the very organizational structure of corporate governance. As Bruce Mac Laury, president of Brookings, observed in his introduction to the colloquium on Blair's work, "The growing gap between winners and losers in lifetime incomes, the continuing human (and human capital) costs of wholesale corporate restructurings . . ." are among the reasons we need this kind of reassessment.[22]

## GOING THE EXTRA MILE

Blair and others who advocate some form of stakeholder capitalism recognize the need to make changes in the law to enable corporate accountability to a variety of stakeholders. It is also the case, however, that many current laws do mandate consideration of stakeholders by businesses and corporations. Coming to mind are the myriad regulations that protect people's health, the health of the environment, the right to organize, and the right to equal opportunity, and those that promote safety at work and in the use of products. These may not constitute the type of wealth-sharing or investment-protecting stakeholder theory reviewed here, but they do act as a reminder of how society and law are capable of responding to the ways business and industry influence the lives of all people. Legal innovations in favor of stakeholder capitalism are seemingly just as possible.

In the meantime, stakeholder capitalism will likely develop as more and more leaders and constituencies are willing to "go the extra mile."

Going the extra mile is simply a metaphor Jesus employed to teach that Christian love goes beyond what the law requires, even when the law can be burdensome. As justice in God's eyes is the servant of mercy, so is law the servant of love. Compliance with the law serves the ends of love, assuming that the laws are just. But love is ready to go beyond compliance to generosity and, where possible, work for laws that can serve the ends of love more fully. Love goes the extra mile.

Although Christian love might seem a strange concept to trot out in a meeting of top management or the board of directors, it is not without its cousins in actual business practice. Lynn Sharp Paine, in a widely read article in the *Harvard Business Review* several years back, advocated an approach to organizational integrity that bears a family resemblance to the ethics of going the extra mile. Paine contrasted businesses that developed an ethos in which ethical conduct was integral to all aspects of day-to-day activities, the integrity model, with those that looked upon ethics as simply a matter of complying with the law, the compliance model.[23]

In the former case, ethical conduct is a positive, welcome feature of organizational life. The corporate ethos has a leavening effect. In a compliance model, conformity to external standards is the basic orientation rather than an internalized ethic. It is an ethic driven more by the avoidance of bad consequences than by good possibilities. In the integrity model, on the other hand, one senses a kind of openness to the good.

As Christians promoting sharing society in general and the promise of stakeholder capitalism in particular, connecting with proposals like Paine's and the companies that exemplify them in practice is a vital point of contact for social dialogue about values and economic life. Kindred concepts in public discourse make Christian contributions about sharing more readily shareable.

## BEYOND THE MORAL MINIMUM: BEYOND OURSELVES

*Cooperation, coalition, solidarity, sufficiency, sustainability, stakeholder theory, community*— all of these terms point in some way to the fact that individuals, institutions, and even nations are involved in a web of relationships with others who also have concerns, interests, and needs. It is an involvement that makes sharing imperative.

When we just spoke of going the extra mile, we were speaking about going beyond what is often referred to as the "moral minimum." The *moral minimum,* to "do no harm," is often construed as compliance with the law. To respect the moral minimum is essential and can demand a lot of people and organizations. It can be a community-minded outlook. It can also be an approach to self-obligation that seeks to do simply what is least required in order to feel free to concentrate on one's individual agenda.

Certainly, the ethics of going the extra mile or going beyond the moral minimum goes beyond the individual. It propels us into the web of relationships with eyes open to the interests, concerns, and needs of others. In a real sense, going beyond ourselves is recognizing and embracing our limits in community with others and thereby exceeding our limitations, the limitations of the very self-centeredness associated with sin.

In this sense, going beyond ourselves is a possibility that exists because there is someone, beyond ourselves, who creates that possibility. Whenever we move beyond ourselves as people, the creating hand of God's grace is at work. We place no limits to the scope of God's grace; it would be impious to do so.

## QUESTIONS FOR DISCUSSION

1. Can you think of examples from your own knowledge or experience where stakeholder analysis would have been helpful and desirable?
2. Can you relate examples from your own knowledge and experience that illustrate the practice of stakeholder capitalism?
3. Think of a local industry. Who are the stakeholders in this company?
4. Think about possible conflicting claims on the part of all stakeholders, such as employees, customers, the local community, the environment, and shareholders. What things should management take into consideration in trying to weigh and balance these claims?

# 8
# TEACH YOUR CHILDREN WELL

O NE OF THE FIRST THINGS WE TEACH OUR CHILDREN when they begin to play with other children is that they should share and, similarly, to take turns. From early on, parents and teachers socialize children to be fair and not selfish.

In her recent book *The Overspent American*, Juliet Schor reports on economist Robert Frank's thoughts about why so many resist the idea that they are "keeping up with the Joneses" or that they are in any way envious of the wealth of others. Frank says that from early childhood, people are taught to be generous and ready to share, and to suppress feelings of jealousy or revenge. Both one-upmanship and anger at defeat are discouraged. And, by adulthood, most people have perfected their ability to cover up or disguise these unsavory sentiments. The problem is, from childhood on, people have been getting mixed signals. Along with the encouragement of generosity, adults in the United States have been socialized to competition and acquisition. In this wide-open consumer society, conspicuous consumption or flaunting the luxuries of success attracts relatively little censure.[1]

The work of Schor and others on the subject of consumption will be discussed presently. For the moment, however, I want to make special note of the ways social, or moral, character is shaped by contradictory values. The policies we may adopt, the economic philosophy we choose to follow, and the way in which we define our obligations toward one another are all a function of character, the vision and impulses that emerge from our life together and shape our ethical orientation and inclination. We cannot cover all aspects of the subject of character here, certainly, but we can say enough to open this important part of the conversation. As is befitting a book on the ethos of economic life, we start with a look at the impact of consumerism on our personal and corporate character.

## CHARACTER AND THE CULTURE OF CONSUMPTION

Some years ago, a pastor friend of mine used to speak of what he called "middle-class sins." He was referring to the consumer lifestyle of the middle class that lures its members, almost unsuspectingly, into overspending and overextending their financial obligations to the point that they have few discretionary funds to use for good causes and those in need. These people did not start out on a path of self-centered greed, but they ended up in a situation where they are guilty of a kind of de facto greedy behavior. It is a situation in which they are now almost economically powerless to change.

This captivity is reflected in Schor's findings that the intensification of competitive spending, a hallmark of consumerism, is resulting in a deterioration of public goods. Locked in a pattern of private spending, people feel they have less and are willing to give less to education, social services, public safety, recreation, and cultural development. More and more, people would rather buy these services for their children in private schools and commercial play areas than contribute to public spaces and programs. Bearing the self-generated financial pressures that they do, many Americans are disinclined to support programs for the poor. "Coupled with dramatic declines in the earning power of these latter groups, the result has been a substantial increase in poverty, the deterioration of poor neighborhoods, and alarming levels of crime and drug use."[2]

The Public Broadcasting System's recent production *Affluenza* makes many of the same points. As citizens have been turned into consumers by marketing, during the last twenty years, the passage of school levies has dropped off and participation in charitable organizations has declined measurably. In poor communities, the sense of deprivation is intense, contributing to crime and other social ills. The greed and consumerism of the affluent, then, not only contribute to the disparities of economic life already observed in this book but also have a subversive effect on the cultural ethos of those who can't compete.[3]

According to Cornel West, the impact of consumerism on African American culture provides a case in point. The aggressive marketing of goods and pleasure within poor, African American communities has had a corrosive effect on their traditional nonmarket values of love, care, and service to others. The predominance of materialistic consumerism "among those living in poverty-ridden conditions, with a limited capacity to ward off self-contempt and self-hatred, results in the possible triumph of the nihilistic threat in black America."[4]

Although such a commitment to spending and consumption may be a sign of flawed character, does it necessarily qualify as greed? I have already suggested that it can lead to a situation whose consequences are de facto those of greed. Further evidence suggests that consumerism contributes to the disparities already noted as a by-product of greed. At the beginning of this book, I associated greed with excess, excessive self-concern and excessive self-aggrandizement, both of which drive wedges deep into community. Also discussed earlier, greed can involve not only the hoarding of money and goods but also the hoarding of power and prestige. Consumerism not only contributes to the conditions for social inequalities, it represents a display of self-aggrandizement and the competitive drive for power and prestige that are associated with greed.

Schor reports that the status gained from acquired possessions, especially the prestigious brands and labels, still remains a powerful force in our culture, despite some evidence of ambiguity over our consumer lifestyle. Furthermore, she states, we establish our identity and worth by the things we buy. "Recent research suggests that the more we have, the more powerful, confident, and socially validated we feel." These convictions are compounded by being drawn into another cultural condition for the emergence of greed, the conviction that the economy can and should always grow, limitlessly. We get caught on a consumer escalator; as the economy grows, the pressures to spend grow along with it. Rising incomes create pressures to spend more in order to keep up with our peers among the emerging wealthy.[5]

The creeping influence of consumerism that captivates our lives and insidiously divides us from one another is part of the phenomenon of greed, even though all who are caught in its web are not the sort of people we normally think of as greedy. The way in which this unself-conscious greed is so tightly woven into the fabric of our society is simply inescapable.

Recalling the legend of King Midas—his wish to turn everything into gold led to great wealth but also to great despair when even his family was transformed into lifeless, precious metal at his touch—

points to a disquieting connection between our "affluenza" and Midas's greed. The PBS documentary pointed out that we spend far more time shopping than we do playing with our children. Moreover, the stresses of overspending and meeting those demands through overwork, or the stresses of failing to meet financial obligations despite overwork, have an obvious negative effect on the family. Many probably started out wanting to have more for the sake of their family's happiness and well-being, but, as in the Midas story, it went too far and the sense of family may have been lost in the process.

Teach your children well, as the Crosby, Stills, and Nash lyrics wisely suggest. And most parents do try to teach their children to share and play fair. Meanwhile, there is a huge marketing strategy afoot to zero in on children, to make consumers of them at an early age. Children are a critical target for companies who not only want to sell them child products but want to get them attached to brands and hooked on competitive buying as soon as possible. An interview with several young teenage girls during the *Affluenza* program is enough to make the point. These girls reported that if they were seen in "off brand," less-expensive sneakers instead of the expensive shoes in fashion, they would be ridiculed. Parents surveyed for the program said their children weren't materialistic; they were "very materialistic." Schor agrees. Parental complaints about their children's consumerism are widespread.[6]

Of course, part of the problem of shaping children's inclinations in the direction of a less-acquisitive lifestyle is that many parents tend to be part of the problem. They give their children money and things not only to please them but also to satisfy their own drive to "keep up." Though children are an extension of their parents' wishes and desires, they often go their parents one better.[7]

In many respects, reports such as these simply confirm what we already know. Furthermore, we also tend to feel some of the same ambiguity and discomfort many feel in the face of our consumeristic world. Many want to change but feel caught in the vortex of a consumer society.

## THE CHARACTER AND VIRTUES OF LOVE

The PBS documentary and Schor's book go on to relate stories of people who have turned away from their consumerist ways and embraced a simpler lifestyle. These are important examples. They are living resources that show what is possible. They are joined by a spate of literature promoting downscaled living and the quest for meaning to life in the midst of shallow consumerism. In considering such resources for change, however, care needs to exercised.

The stimulus for change is often presented in terms of greater personal happiness. People who tell their stories of rejecting materialist concerns certainly show a sensitivity to other of life's values: richer relationships, more leisure, less stress, and so on. But the primary appeal is that this wider range of values will bring greater happiness. Nothing wrong with that. It leads to some admirable examples. Yet, there is a danger that the appeal to greater happiness will be reduced to just another personal choice, a matter of prudence or preference. In that form, it lacks moral force.

Of course, one can always point out that not only are we happier when we cut back but the future of the environment demands it. Fair enough. But this, too, is an argument from prudence. Doubtless it is a good argument, and an urgent one. Still, as discussed in a previous chapter, arguing against consumption on the basis of environmental limits and economic justice will likely fall prey to alternative readings of the salient scientific and geopolitical data.

Compelling and persuasive moral arguments are needed. Practical appeals to satisfaction and prudence are important. They can be instrumental in effecting deeper shifts in the public ethos. Nevertheless, they do not guarantee a higher level of sharing.

## NEIGHBOR LOVE

The fact that the love Jesus taught—love our neighbors as ourselves—has retained the name "neighbor love" is not insignificant. "Love" and "neighbor" stand in complementary and inseparable relation to one another. Both convey the inextricable relatedness of human existence qualified by the utter necessity of caring and sharing as the lifeblood of our way of being.

To repeat an earlier theme, we are both formed and informed by love in the Christian life and ethic. Being formed by love is the manner in which character is shaped in the Christian life. Being informed by love refers to the way in which neighbor love gives direction to our ethical decisions. For the present, the former is of concern.

In Romans 12:2, Paul says, "Do not be conformed to this world, but be transformed by the renewing of your minds, so that you may discern what is the will of God—what is good and acceptable and perfect." In writing to the Philippians, Paul calls upon them to have the "mind of Christ" who, "though he was in the form of God, did not regard equality with God as something to be exploited, but emptied himself, taking the form of a slave" (Philippians 2:5-7). In both passages, the form or shape of the Christian life is Christ himself. In Romans it is implicit, and in Philippians it is explicit. In both statements, Paul is speaking of our formation in Christ as involving the mind. The mind shaped by Christ's own love is the core of what we mean by Christian character. It signals an outlook on life and a disposition toward it that is reflective of the love Christ portrayed in his person and his teaching.[8]

A further understanding of the character of love is afforded in considering the virtues or traits of character that give it definition. We have really been discussing several of these along the way. Generosity and readiness to share are reflective of Jesus' own self-giving love for us. Generosity and readiness to share recognize our inherent relatedness and the obligations that flow from that reality. The principles of sustainability, sufficiency, and solidarity that have surfaced in our reflections certainly stand in close relationship to generosity and readiness to share. Like those virtues of love, these principles participate in the other-directedness of neighbor love.

If we search further for virtues that could express the character of love in ways specific to our present concern, there is one other worth considering. That virtue is frugality.

## NEIGHBOR LOVE AND THE VIRTUE OF FRUGALITY

For many, frugality has connoted a kind of penny-pinching approach to life, often with the purpose of saving money in order to build wealth. In this form, frugality is not a particularly attractive trait. Of course, frugality can also be a practice born of economic necessity rather than a trait of character. The need to "make do" under the pressure of severely limited financial circumstances may drive people into frugality without any moral commitment on their part. Whether a trait of character or a function of necessity, however, frugality has often been associated with individual behavior and personal choice, having little to do directly with larger social goals. In

short, frugality has not fared particularly well in popular consciousness. To make matters worse, in affluent societies, it simply seems
old-fashioned, part of a less-prosperous era.

Ethicist James Nash has done a convincing job of rehabilitating
this venerable old virtue from the sorts of distortions just mentioned.
Frugality is a way of moderation in the handling of material wealth.
It rejects the notion that people are insatiable in their drive for material wealth and pleasure. It resists the culture of "more" and strives
to deal with the psychological and social dynamics that stimulate
overconsumption. At the level of public policy, frugality stands
against the ideology of unlimited growth. It is concerned that there
be enough for all, both in terms of the just distribution of wealth and
in the preservation of the environment and its resources. It is not a
purely individualistic pursuit.[9] In some respects, this version of frugality bears a strong family resemblance to Christian concepts of
stewardship.

Frugality is a helpful term in this context because its frame of ref-
erence is economic life. It signals a lifestyle quite different from greed
and consumerism. And, as Nash develops it, frugality is a player in
the struggle for responsible use of resources throughout human society. Nash relates it directly to the character of Christian love:

> Frugality in classical Christian ethical interpretations is an expression
> of love seeking the good or well-being of others in response to their
> needs and to the God who is love. The source of the sacrificial dimen-
> sion in frugality is love of neighbor, for love always entails giving up
> at least some of our self-interests and benefits for the sake of the wel-
> fare of others in communal relationships.[10]

In the consumer world of affluent societies and affluent elites,
frugality seems like a square peg in a round hole. At times, we almost
feel as though it is our duty to consume: "What will happen to the
nation's economic health if I don't do my part for the annual
Christmas shopping spree so vital to our retail industry and all the
jobs it provides?" Nash understands this. That is why he calls frugality a "subversive virtue." Sudden mass conversions to frugality
would cause no end of grief in the markets with dire consequences.
Despite that completely improbable turn of events, however, the
moderate course of frugality in pursuit of a sharing society could just
as easily be the harbinger of a more stable and just economic order
with a truly sustainable future.

## NEIGHBOR LOVE AND COMMUNITARIAN VIRTUES

Community and a communitarian spirit stand in contrast to the predominant individualism of our society. A sharing society stands in contrast to the presuppositions and effects of greed. It is characteristic of love that it seeks unity and community, wholeness rather than fragmentation. Paul Tillich, one of the great theologians of the twentieth century, has described the meaning of Christian love as "the reunification of the separated." The love of God in Christ has brought us back together with God and one another in Christ. Christian love seeks to do the same. Those virtues of neighbor love, which embody a keen awareness of mutuality and a strong drive toward the building of community, might well be dubbed the communitarian virtues of neighbor love.

Several of the virtues that surface in the Beatitudes at the beginning of the Sermon on the Mount (Matthew 5:1-12) seem to be good candidates. Poverty of spirit projects a lack of pretense and self-concern necessary for the kind of openness to neighbors and their needs that is essential to an inclusive and caring community. Mercy with its compassionate regard for the suffering of others is the foundation of biblical justice and the keystone of genuine community. Peacemaking is a virtue and a practice of reconciliation, which mirrors God's reconciling work in Christ (2 Corinthians 5:19) and brings together again those who were estranged. All these are essential aspects of love in its striving for community.

We have talked about community as an idea encompassing our essential relatedness to one another and the values and obligations that flow from that reality. We have talked about community as a word for concern and involvement with others in contrast to individualism. We have talked of community in terms of complex alliances of cooperation for the development of a more just global economic order and to deal with issues of hunger and the environment. We have talked about community as an active sense of mutuality in contrast to selfish greed on the part of individuals or groups. We have talked about community in terms of sharing rather than hoarding basic goods or power and privilege. We have worked with the notion of community in all these different ways, not to the detriment of individual freedom or a free market economy, but with the aim of calling upon one another to use our freedom in support of one another. Do we need to say more about "community"?

There has certainly been a great deal of talk about the subject of community in the wake of all the studies underscoring our individualistic culture and growing isolation from one another. As one might expect, then, much of the discussion has lamented the loss of community and the threat such a loss poses to the social ethos. Will the dissipation of community drive us deeper into selfish individualism and greater alienation from one another?

Years after the work of Robert Bellah and his colleagues charted the ways in which individualism has eroded community, folks are still nodding their heads in assent when his findings are rehearsed. Ethicist Larry Rasmussen has tracked the way in which the "acids of modernity" have dissolved the basic forms of community that once provided moral formation.[11] Wendell Berry has deplored the erosion of rural communities and the erosion of the land that he believes is sure to follow when those responsible for it don't live together on it.[12]

More recently, John F. Freie, a political scientist, has published a book in which he speaks of "counterfeit communities," arrangements that give the illusion of community but are not at all authentic. Freie explains that people have such a deep and frustrated need to be connected that they are vulnerable to these counterfeit versions of community. His study leads to the irony that the financial forces of consumerism, which have been instrumental in the dismantling of traditional forms of community, are now in the business of marketing community in ersatz forms. Planned housing enclaves, malls, and phony neighborhood *Cheers* bars located in airports are just a few examples of a "manufactured" community.[13]

As one would expect, you have to know what the genuine article looks like in order to identify what is counterfeit. Freie has a description to go by, as do many others who concern themselves with this matter. Authentic community for him includes a number of features resembling some covered in the discussion here: just relationships, active participation and cooperation among all, a sense of caring about others, and a feeling for the spirit of connectedness, to name the most prominent (Freie, 23).

It is important to be able to spot a fake, so it is important to be clear about the marks of true community. However, it is also important in this ever changing world to recognize the need to appreciate and support a variety of human interactions that manifest values of community. In quest of a full range of ideas and meanings associated with *community*, I turned to my thesaurus. It led me to an impressive array of relational concepts, including cooperation, collaboration, teamwork, mutuality, alliance, work together, pull together, stand together. These are the type of relational dynamics identified herein as a counterpoint to the purely self-serving activities of greed. Community has a number of life-forms, but the moral DNA common to them all is the kind of regard for one another inherent in neighbor love. It means not only respecting one another's rights but also responding to one another's needs.

Many different kinds of communities, or even partial realizations of community in many different settings, are needed to keep the values of sharing and mutual concern alive in the public consciousness. For Christians, it is a matter of practicing and promoting the virtues of love's character in all venues of human interaction and encouraging whatever is congenial from outside the pale of the faith. The virtues of generosity, openness to one's neighbor, compassionate justice, and solidarity with those in need combine forces to keep people together when the power of greed and the influence of consumerism threaten separation.

Not only do such virtues help to bring about some realization of community, but community is the context in which such virtues are developed and nurtured. The stories or traditions and the values they express, which are the foundation for so many communities, are the seedbed of character and virtue.

## TELLING STORIES

For Christians, character and virtue, although nurtured by discipline, developed by knowledge, and encouraged by example, are always a gift of grace rather than a personal, moral achievement. The channel of this grace is the story told and retold in word and sacrament, each and every time the Christian community gathers, throughout time and space. It is the story of God's love in Jesus Christ. Through this story, God's grace is operative, awakening faith and creating the community of faith we call the church. Through this story, the Holy Spirit is at work to shape a people for the witness of love in a world riddled with enmity and division.

The story of the Christ provides a lens through which to look at other stories and to discern in them what is good and true and deserving of support. Moreover, the myriad stories that spring from the fertile soil of human interaction often add texture to the understanding of the day-to-day, incarnate meaning of the Christ story.

What might these stories look like? There is no want of stories surrounding great figures of history and towering examples of the faith who gave their all for the love of God and neighbor. It is also important, I think, to lift up stories from ordinary life experience, lest we think that virtue is the province of a rare few.

Some of these stories will emerge from families. For me, the story of my great-aunt and godmother, Ida Mott, comes to mind. She was a person of strong faith and total lack of pretense. In her flat above a hardware store, where she lived more than fifty years with my Uncle Tom, she taught piano to more than a generation in Elkhorn, Wisconsin. The children came in an endless stream up the steep steps to her dining room studio not because she was the only teacher in the area, or the cheapest. They came because she gave them more than piano lessons. She gave them love. She was completely free in her faith and full of fun. She shared herself and everything she had with her pupils, neighbors, church, and family so completely that no one whose life she touched was ever quite the same again. While Aunt Ida was alive, the family was never out of touch with the ways of Jesus. Now it is important that her story and others like it be remembered and told so that from its generative power new stories can be born.

Out of communities of faith come communities of caring whose activities and spirit become a story to be told. In India, many years ago, I met a group of nuns who were attending a workshop in which I had a part as a guest instructor. These young women had dedicated their lives to caring for the dying in a small rural hospital. It was really a hospice, for there were few medical resources, only simple forms of comfort care. Day in and day out, they gave their lives to comfort the dying. They had no victories to celebrate, only the hope of their faith. As I came to know them in casual conversation and more serious moments of sharing, I learned more from them about the truth of joyful service in Christ than anything they could possibly have gotten from my lectures. Too much self-giving can turn into an unhealthy passion for self-denial, but in these women, I experienced a rich blend of robust humor, peacefulness, and a great capacity for enthusiasm and excitement, all signs of vitality. Theirs is a story to be told and a spirit to be emulated.

Congregations are "storied communities" as well. Not only are they constituted by the story, but on its foundation they receive the grace to build their own narrative. An example of this is Love Zion Baptist Church in Columbus, Ohio. With the modest means of a few hundred members, this congregation has put together a program of social ministry to community children, families, and people with disabilities. Love Zion represents the type of sharing and caring that has been emblematic of African American Christianity. There are innumerable examples of this type of congregational ministry across all denominational lines. Certainly, there are also similar activities of service going on in communities of other faiths.

These tales of community outreach take their place beside the stories of what are now vast networks of social service, such as Catholic Charities or Lutheran Services in America. As integral parts of their church's mission, these organizations operate hospitals, long-term-care facilities, family services, ex-offender programs, homes for the developmentally disabled, adoption services, food pantries, and so on. Beyond service, they also serve the needs of the total population by engaging in public advocacy for justice.

Within these vast networks, there are inspiring stories of small groups of people who early in the life of these churches saw unmet needs and rallied the meager resources of local congregations to try to meet those needs. Those early efforts have snowballed through the years to become the wide-reaching organizations of today. There are also stories of people of diverse faiths coming together in common service through these organizations, including how their good stewardship of the public funds entrusted to them has been a leaven in society. These stories must be told over and over so that dedication can be rekindled in each new generation.

Not all stories come out of families or communities of faith, however. They may also reside in contexts as seemingly improbable as the workplace. John Freie has argued that efforts at building community in the workplace almost always result in a counterfeit community. Even programs of employee self-management do not mitigate this judgment. The pressures of profit maximization and the inevitable concentration of power in top management make true participatory community illusory (Freie, 77–97).

With no less realism than Freie, however, Stewart Herman, a Christian ethicist who has worked extensively in business ethics, wants to affirm those stories in industry where a healthy balance of "managerial prerogative, employee self-representation, and employee self-management" has been achieved. These are essential elements in a "covenantal" approach to business ethics. Herman sees this exemplified in the well-known Saturn experiment by General Motors. However flawed the experiment may be, even however short-lived its successes, the Saturn story supports a conviction with which Herman operates: "God works through every kind of human relationship to bring the whole human commonwealth into covenantal relations of mutual respect, care, and justice. No sphere of human life, not even the most hard-nosed business enterprise, is immune to God's influence or lies beyond God's claim."[14]

Stories of a covenantal approach to management coupled with stories of businesses respectful of the communities in which they are located and responsible in their treatment of the environment need to be told. They may be only incomplete or fragmentary realizations of the values of community, but they are the building blocks for new traditions and healthier corporate cultures. That people are working at such arrangements against strong odds is a story to be told in itself. Christians will want to help shape such stories and lift them up in the face of the kind of facile cynicism with which people excuse themselves from working for positive change.

Ford Motor Company has a new vision for positive change. Under the leadership of new CEO Jacques Nasser, Ford has launched a companywide education program. Most of the positive change being sought is the development of new leadership skills that will make Ford a more competitive global corporation. There is also a community service component in the new Ford curriculum, however. Every employee must log some time in community service. Ford wants to be a world-class corporate citizen, Nasser explains, which means more than contributing money. It entails involvement in the communities where Ford operates.

> Ford people have built schools in Mexico, worked with the homeless in New York, and cared for the elderly in Hong Kong. Our people have worked side by side with community activists under the most daunting circumstances. One organization that teaches our people a lot is Focus: HOPE in Detroit. It distributes food to about 80,000 people a month and trains young people in all sorts of life and job skills.[15]

Is community service really significant? Won't it simply be
smothered under an avalanche of other job performance expectations? Is it just another instance of a greedy corporation throwing a
sop to the community, tooting its own horn, and doing nothing that
prompts genuine systemic change? There is plenty of evidence in the
history of business that might lead one to say yes to these questions.
One must be realistic, but one must also tell the story of the effort
and pray for its possibilities.

Stories belong to professional communities also. Certainly the
story of medicine has had a long and honorable history. It is a story
of dedication to patients and an unflagging fight against disease and
death. More recently, it has begun to blend into its story a new
understanding of care for the dying and modesty in the face of life's
limits. It is seeking to recover the best of its traditions of compassion.
It is a story that will be enriched by those medical professionals who
work to resist features of the health care system that fail to provide
appropriate care or fail to provide any care at all. The story of medicine is also a story woven together with the golden threads of its sub-
stories. These are the real dramas of those who give the best of care
under the worst of circumstances, often giving up greater financial
rewards and career advancement to bring medicine to areas of
poverty here and abroad in urban centers and rural outposts.

To all these examples from business and professional life could
be added accounts of civic solidarity in the face of emergency and
exigency. And who has not been heartened by the outpouring of
donations to communities all over the world overtaken by flood,
earthquake, or some other disaster? In such times of dire need, stories abound of regular people who travel great distances to help.
One can be skeptical and say that such splurges of sharing in the context of crisis are atypical, that they are but fleeting remnants of a
largely lost community spirit. No matter how difficult it is to sustain
patterns of generosity, these neighborly actions are authentic
impulses deep within the human spirit. They serve as a reminder
that there is a reservoir of caring, despite all the manifestations of
self-serving greed.

So many different expressions of community are out there. With
them we discover many different stories that give life to the values of
sharing and caring that are the very foundation of community. They
are uneven in their quality. Some are inspiring, while others are

clearly imperfect and incomplete. Some will have enduring power and remain in our memories, fueling our aspirations, while others will come and go, their influence fleeting. Nevertheless, all are important as adjuncts to the story. They find their full meaning when drawn into the orbit of God's story for us. They contribute to the development and understanding of the communal virtues.

For Christians, these stories are a point of contact for getting across the values they hold dear. They remind us that God is at work in the world. Indeed, these narratives remind us that there are many ways in which we are a sharing society. Sharing is the enemy of greed. Teach your children well. Tell them stories. Find communities for them in which they can experience the sorts of values and people who will become their stories.

## QUESTIONS FOR DISCUSSION

1. How do you experience the impact of consumerism on your life and your commitments?
2. How would you describe the impact consumerism is having on our children? Is it making them a greedy generation? How can we work with them and help them?
3. Do you have stories to share?
4. In what ways can the church be a community in which communitarian virtues can take root and flourish?

# 9
# A QUESTION OF CALLING

NOT TOO MANY MONTHS AFTER THE Public Broadcasting System broadcast *Affluenza,* with its critical analysis of our consumer society, ABC News aired a new and somewhat more sympathetic look at greed, *Greed with John Stossel.*[1] In a statement no doubt intended for the sort of shock value guaranteed to grab people's attention, philosopher David Kelley offered the opinion that convicted inside trader and junk bond king Michael Milken did more for the world than Mother Teresa. Outrageous and offensive as this statement is, it is really only a bit of hyperbole for the theme that runs through the program. Beside Kelley, Ted Turner and economist Walter Williams combined to make the familiar argument that greed, competitive self-interest, has made this a better world through the creation of wealth and better products and services.

This argument also relies on the conviction that new wealth is constantly being created, that possibilities are limitless. Therefore, if one person gains great wealth, it does not mean as a direct consequence that someone else has less or not enough. These proponents of "greed" also submit that nonprofit services, supposedly motivated by caring, are far less effective and reliable than for-profit firms providing the same services. Given the assumption that all people act out of self-interest, it follows that giving good service in any field is rewarded by financial success. This becomes our real and effectual motive for serving our neighbor. These arguments give the appearance of a highly problematic, unreconstructed form of egoism: we are all in it for ourselves, and the world works better when we work with that premise.

Philosophers and theologians alike have had serious problems with this approach for many years now. It is a caricature of Adam Smith. The self-interest model cannot even be consistently sustained in actual business practice, as respected business ethicist Laura Nash has convincingly shown.[2] Beyond that, the definition of greed seems to make no distinction between healthy ambition integrated with other values and pure, selfish ambition. Finally, it does not face seriously the reality of limits in environmental resources or the amount of suffering in this out-of-whack world.

It is probably a good thing not to make too much of a television program like this one, which is not capable of a carefully nuanced discussion of the issues. Nonetheless, despite its conceptual flaws, it does provide a reminder of the benefits so many people enjoy from the financial successes and new developments of the free market system. The argument might also hold, in some areas of the world, that even the poor are better off than the poor of previous generations. Furthermore, some would argue, when challenged with global economic disparities, the global spread of capitalism and its high-tech products will enable poor countries to leapfrog generations of economic and technological development as they begin to catch up.

So it is that we often feel caught in the tight grip of profound ambiguity. Our capitalist system, in one form or another, has proven the most successful economic arrangement of the common era. The benefits have been many. At the same time, it has become the handy tool of selfish individualism and greed to the detriment of community values and the health of nature. Selfishness and refusal to confront either limits or limitations have played a key role in creating the disparities discussed here. So great is the power of the market that it has led in many ways to the "commodification" of life.

Just the other day, I opened an envelope containing my periodic pension account statement. It told me that my choice to invest most of my funds in stocks had paid off handsomely in the recent bull market. Here I was, celebrating my gains while still working away on a book manuscript dealing with greed! I can make the case that I chose to put my money in a portfolio of companies screened for their social responsibility. That helps, I suppose. I can also point out that my holdings are rather modest when compared to the holdings of many others; mine is not the portfolio of a wealthy person at all. (I would not want to make that claim against more than two-thirds of the world, however.) I could go on to talk about my charitable contributions, if that would help. Even if I were able to successfully portray myself as a generous person of modest means, however, the fact remains that I am a full participant in our economic system and have some responsibility for how it works. I cannot escape the grip of its often confusing and vexing choices or its glaring inequities. I am obliged to deal with it as responsibly as I am able. I cannot abdicate involvement in the ethical issues of economic life by simply saying that this is the way of life in a sinful world.

There was probably a time—a time that still is for some Christians—when I and others like me would feel relatively untroubled by questions of our complicity in an unjust economic order and our responsibility to promote positive change. Provided that our money was come by honestly, it would have been mainly a matter of thanking God for prosperity and exercising good and generous stewardship. As John Wesley said in his well-known sermon "On the Use of Money," "Gain all you can. Save all you can. Give all you can."[3] Looking deeper into the phenomenon of greed and the way it seeps into the pores of every appendage of corporate life, however, it becomes clear that this is a major item on the vocational agenda for God's people. It is not only a matter of personal stewardship, it is also a question of the social witness of the church to which we are called as individuals and as a community of faith.

In many respects, the entire discussion in this book has been a consultation on how we go about our Christian calling when confronted with the diversified manifestations of greed. Rather than attempt a summary, I want to try to draw together some of the most important, fundamental messages discovered along the way and concentrate them in four theses on our vocation as Christian people.

## THESIS ONE: OUR CALL TO COMBAT GREED

The call to combat greed is a personal call, to be sure. And, participating in the formation of public policy and in the shaping of economic life is a genuine part of our call to witness to the Gospel.

In baptism we are ordained into the priesthood of all believers, into the ministry of the whole people of God. As Peter put the matter in 1 Peter 2:9, ". . . you are a chosen race, a royal priesthood, a holy nation, God's own people, in order that you may proclaim the mighty acts of him who called you out of darkness into his marvelous light." All of God's people have a vocation, a divine call to proclaim the good news of God's salvation in Jesus, the Christ. It has not always been clear to Christian people what sorts of activities are included in answering that call, however.

Certainly, all in the church have been clear that evangelism, proclaiming the good news, is at the heart of it all. But is concern for justice, peace, and the common good included in this call? Answers have differed, but more often than not, distinctions have been drawn between involvement in the affairs of secular society and the endeavor of converting people to faith and nurturing them in that faith. God wants Christians to be concerned with justice, peace, and the common good. God commands us to love our neighbors. This is how individual Christians should behave in the world, however; it is not integral to the primary evangelical mission and vocation of the church.

This distinction congealed into what was more like a separation during the later development of Luther's "two kingdoms" doctrine, as briefly discussed in chapter 3 with his account of God's left-hand and right-hand modes of rule. As a consequence, many generations of Lutherans operated on the premise that they should love their neighbors and be good citizens in accordance with God's command under the left-hand rule. The heart of Christianity, however, under God's right-hand rule, was to be found in one's personal faith and life within the church, and one's witness to the word of salvation outside the church.

Christians, then, received little guidance from the church in matters of justice and the common good and the church. As an organization, the church kept its hands off. Such pursuits were largely the task of leaders within the orders of government, and the economy, which God has providentially established. The church has no special advice to offer in matters of secular concern. Its best influence comes when good Christian people in government and business set a good example. Indeed, there has been a lingering fear that, if the church were to become socially active, its gospel mission would be confused with a program of social reform.

While a quietistic reaction to social activism describes what happened among Luther's heirs, it is not exclusively a development of Lutheranism. Other Protestant denominations also kept social issues at arm's length. Furthermore, this tendency to separate one's faith life from public life and work life has been reinforced in America by the forces of secularization in our culture and our customary notions of the "separation of church and state."

While there are certainly good theological reasons for distinguishing the hope God promises in Jesus from the best we can hope for from the world, there are also good theological reasons for seeing that our work in the world for justice, peace, and the good of the whole creation is a way of pointing to the hope of God's promise as well. That is, there are reasons for asserting that the Christian witness in working for a better world is a genuine ingredient of our evangelism. As such, working against the deleterious effects of greed and the cultural assumptions that feed that avarice is part of our Christian calling to "proclaim the marvelous deeds of him who called [us] out of darkness into his marvelous light." (1 Peter 2:9) How is this so?

A clue comes from previous remarks about being a "people of anticipation." This theme is based on our hope for God's promised future. Jesus' victory over sin and death is a victory of broad proportions. It is a victory for the wholeness and harmony of all creation, which Paul says will "be set free from its bondage to decay" (Romans 8:21). It will be a peaceable kingdom, as the prophet Isaiah foresaw, in which the wolf shall lie down with the lamb. It is a victory of life over death, for the wholeness of life and the wholeness of the human community in intimate unity with God. This means the death of death, the triumph of health, the end of injustice and indignity, the triumph of equality, the end of hunger, the joy of the feast at God's table, the downfall of enmity, and the ascendancy of peace. These components of the promised future were discussed at the end of chapters 2 and 4.

To work toward these promised values in direct opposition to the impulses and products of greed is to proclaim the hope of the gospel in its broadest proportions. This is our vocation. Our various occupations, which can include parenting, work life, public service, volunteer service, and the responsibilities of citizenship, become avenues through which we can express our vocation of Christian witness.

Looking at our occupation and the financial rewards we gain as means of service to our family and our neighbors in the world, rather than merely our path to material success, shows the types of caring and sharing that mitigate the effects of greed and contribute to a more generous cultural character. When we exercise our opportunities to participate in public policy advocacy on behalf of those in need and the relief of unjust disparities, we stand for the values of community over and against rampant individualism. In both cases, we are trying to place the aims of economic life in a larger more comprehensive arena of value.

Even as we strive in hope, we recognize that *hope* points to the future. The promise is present and certain in the triumph of the resurrection. We know how it all turns out. However, as we struggle in the present, we do so with the realism of living in a world that is not yet there. We, as individuals, live with the assurance of God's salvation in Christ while we battle the sin that lingers within us. It is this way with the world, too. So there are reasons to distinguish what God promises for the world's future from the best we can hope for from the world. Nevertheless, we should not separate the activities of our faith from the endeavors of our world. The world, in which we work and witness, is the world God has promised to redeem.

In a sparkling satire entitled "The Market as God" in a recent issue of the *Atlantic Monthly,* renowned Harvard theologian Harvey Cox recalls how he wondered whether or not he, as a theologian, could possibly understand economics and the market. After all, the market has all the features of a religion and can be readily understood by theologians. His biting, amusing satire exposes those who want to make a god of the market rather than making the market subservient to higher and broader values. Near the end of the article, Cox makes a statement worth quoting here:

> There is, however, one contradiction between the religion of The Market and the traditional religions that seems to be insurmountable. All the traditional religions teach that human beings are finite creatures and that there are limits to any earthly enterprise. [For the market,] the First Commandment is "There is *never* enough."[4]

The gospel sets us free from the curse of basing our hope in our own limitless possibilities so that we may enjoy the limitless grace and limitless life of God. Freedom in the promise of life is the foundation of generosity.

## THESIS TWO: OUR CALL TO CHRISTIAN WITNESS

This call, to Christian witness for a sharing society, is a calling of the whole church. Thesis One distilled the theological rationale for saying that the church's witness for a sharing society is an authentic part of the church's gospel mission because the values of wholeness and equity that we seek in a sharing society anticipate those which are part of the promise for the reign of God and which Jesus' revealed in his person and work. If the whole church is involved, what does that mean in practice? Answering that question thoroughly would require at least another book. We can briefly describe some key features, however.

## PREACHING IN THE CHURCH

The theological perspective, advanced here, in which social mission and gospel mission are blended in a single complementary witness needs to be a constant influence on the church's preaching. What is preached, more than anything else, sets the parameters of mission and ministry. If concerns for the social witness of the church are relegated to a single committee or agency or, if they are relegated to an occasional topic in adult education classes, they will remain on the back burner. If they are a regular part of the church's preaching, they will more likely be a regular part of the church's mission.

## THEOLOGICAL EDUCATION

The sorts of concerns addressed throughout this book need to receive strong representation in theological education for the ministries of the church. The curricula of theological schools are crammed full with the basics of a foundational theological education. In the past seminaries admitted students only after they had completed a thorough preseminary program in college. The days when this was the norm are long gone. This means that theological schools must expend most of their energy on building theological and biblical literacy and teaching the basic skills of ministry. Going beyond this basic education to inculcate a deeper understanding and commitment to the church's social ministry requires a special commitment. Seminaries and schools of theology will require the support and encouragement of their constituents if this is to be effective. They cannot do this on their own if the church has no interest beyond its own growth.

## STEWARDSHIP EDUCATION

The church needs to teach a broader type of stewardship, one that points people beyond the needs of the local congregation to a broader mission for sharing their gifts of self and money. Along with this goes a conscious affirmation of the activities and giving Christians engage in on behalf of justice and the needs of their neighbors.

## STEWARDSHIP IN THE CHURCH

Along with a broader view of stewardship practiced by individual Christians there is a companion need to exercise broader stewardship at the level of congregational and churchwide priorities. Will parish committees on social concerns and church departments on church and society receive vigorous support and attention, or remain a side-bar operation with a small piece of the action? How to weight church commitments to addressing issues of economic life in society will be a tough call. After all, a healthy church must be built and maintained before its mission can include the manifold needs of the world. Yet, it may also be the case that a vigorous witness in the midst of the world's affairs, not restricted to personal evangelism, will itself produce a healthy church. Decisions will require serious dialogue within congregations and judicatories as different needs compete for limited resources.

## SUPPORT SOCIAL MINISTRY ORGANIZATIONS

A heightened sense of breadth in the mission of the church is a good platform on which to renew and strengthen ties with church-related social ministry organizations. As noted in the last chapter, these agencies have rich stories of a multitude of services. They are important, concrete expressions of Christian caring and sharing. Many such agencies have outgrown the cozy relationships with churches that marked their beginnings. The expansion of services, the complexity of the modern world, and the professional and other requirements that come with the essential influx of government funds has made these organizations more businesslike, more professionalized, more diverse in their staffing, and bigger than ever. Many feel that these agencies and their founding churches have drifted apart because of these changes. It need not and should not be so. The church needs the ministry of these organizations, and they need the spiritual and moral support of the church. Initiatives to foster communication and dialogue between the church and its social ministry organizations can help recover the vision of social ministry as integral to the overall mission of the church in the world.

## ENGAGE IN ADVOCACY

Many church bodies have permanent staff engaged in advocacy at local, state, and national levels. People who monitor events in the United Nations complement these folks. Through the direct efforts of church "lobbyists," members and congregations are able to communicate with their representatives in government on issues dealing with the types of problems tracked in this book. These would include such issues as improvements in health care delivery, welfare reform, steps to alleviate hunger, protection of the environment, extension of equal rights guarantees, critical decisions on trade policy, budget priorities, and a host of other questions related to inordinate inequities in the distribution of power and money.

People engaged in the church's global mission are important partners with those involved in advocacy. They work together with Christian leaders and churches throughout the world that struggle daily with the deprivation that besets their lands. These working relationships are a source of intimate communication about the reality of disparity, helping to alert everyone about the needs that are out there.

## A TRULY CATHOLIC CHURCH

Catholicity, or universality, is one of the marks of the church. A truly catholic church will seek to live out the fact that God's love in Christ extends to all people. This means a concerted effort to break down barriers of race, class, and gender that are the bedfellows of greed and often the offspring of greedy drives for power and privilege. For those who hold economic advantage and the power that goes with it, exclusion is one effective means of control.

When the church embodies diversity with equality, it makes a strong witness for a sharing society. This can only be enhanced by increased efforts at ecumenical sharing and cooperation. Ecumenical cooperation blends the gifts of various traditions and helps to promote diversity among church bodies that otherwise might find it difficult to break out of their historically ethnic identities.

## A THEOLOGY FOR THE LOVE OF ALL CREATION

With a rich theology of creation and a vision of its wholeness and perfection in the future reign of God, the church has all the tools it needs to fashion a theology for the love of all creation. As discussed in chapter 2, we are created in the image of God to care for the earth as God has cared for it. The basis of our love for creation is God's pronouncement that it is "very good" (Genesis 1:31). The whole of creation possesses an intrinsic value; it is to be honored for its own sake. If the limits of nature are to be protected from the incursions of greed, we will need more than just a utilitarian assessment of whether or not the latest science really supports our fears. Restraint will finally require reverence. The world around us is the work of God's hands and possesses the innate value God has conferred upon it. Communities of faith all over the world have the vocation to evoke reverence for the creation in their theology and make that conviction public by their advocacy.

## A PLACE TO TALK

The world of business can be so demanding in its competitiveness and so harsh in its penalties for failure that people of faith are often pushed to the edge trying to reconcile conscience and the conflicts of work life. They see the effects of greed all around them and fear being compromised by their participation in the corporate world. Congregations and organizations within the church can and should be places where people who are grappling with these moral quandaries can talk to one another. Such mutual consultation and cooperation is a genuine ministry through which Christians can become better equipped to carry out their vocation. We desperately need a place where we can be brutally honest about the things that trouble us. Only then can we begin to make discoveries together about how the word of God addresses us at the intersection of faith and work.

## WE ARE IN IT TOGETHER

The operative word here is *together.* The church is a vast network of Christian people, throughout time and space, knit together as the body of Christ, one body with many members possessing various gifts (Romans 12). There is great comfort and encouragement in this dimension of life in Christ. As discussed in this book, the call to generosity and sharing in witness to the love of Christ, and in opposition to selfishness and greed, is one that engages us at every level of human interaction. It is a daunting, if not overwhelming, task. Therefore, it is vital to remember that the people of God are present at every level of human interaction. We are there with a variety of gifts and opportunities, strengthened by the examples of those who have gone before.

We are in it together; we don't have to go it alone. We have the promise of the future as our beacon and our hope. Along the way, we have the assurance that we are not lacking in any spiritual gift from our faithful God (1 Corinthians 1:7-8) and that God, who began a good work in us, will bring it to completion (Philippians 1:6). What you or I can do as individuals may seem miniscule, but what the whole body of Christ can do in concert provides a strong, living voice.

Most of the items mentioned under this thesis are fit subjects for extensive treatment. I have only enumerated them here with brief comment, but I invite you to connect them with points already made and later pick them up for further conversation and exploration. Taken together, they seem to say that the church not only *has* a mission, the church *is* a mission. What we are and what we do need to be tightly intertwined.

## THESIS THREE: THE CHURCH'S CALL TO WITNESS

The calling of the church to witness is a call for dialogue in our pluralistic world. What we do in the church should prepare us for what we do in the world. What we should be able to expect from one another in the shared faith of the church cannot be taken for granted in the world at large, however. As we chart a course for a sharing society and seek to foster those virtues that strengthen the bonds of togetherness and mutuality, we know that we are doing so in a pluralistic world, a world of staggering diversity. How can we hope to find common foundations on which to build the edifice of a more equitable society in which generosity is cherished and avarice disparaged?

In some respects, this is not a new problem. The world has always been pluralistic in makeup and lacking in moral consensus. We probably feel it more intensely today because we have become a global society and because rational arguments have not resolved all the issues, as many once thought they might. Nonetheless, when we consider the problem of consolidating the moral underpinnings for a just world, we know that many others have charged this hill before us.

Despite setbacks and a realistic recognition that only the power of God—not the possibilities of human progress—can bring us to the promised future, Christians have believed in a divinely ordained basis for seeking the common good despite our diversity. Paul states that the gentiles, who were outside the circle of Israel's faith, "show that what the law requires is written on their hearts, to which their own conscience bears witness" (Romans 2:15). However crippled by the pervasiveness of sin, we have an innate awareness of the right and the good. Roman Catholic natural law tradition embodies this conviction in its belief that there is an innate knowledge of the divine will embedded in the nature of things and accessible to human reason. Lutheran theology talks about "civil righteousness" as the capacity of humankind to understand and do what is right and just. The Reformed tradition, with its roots in Calvin's theology, has held to a strong doctrine of the "sovereignty of God" that sees God at work among believers and nonbelievers alike.

The basic convictions of these traditions seem to be sustained by a number of historical expressions of ethical insight and moral commitment. For example, constitutional provisions in which there are clear protections for human rights and democratic provisions for just government. The United Nations Declaration of Human Rights is in many ways a stunning example of global moral consensus, however uneven its reception among nations. The statement of the Parliament of the World's Religions, "Toward a Global Ethic," is yet another instance of how dialogue, even among doctrinally disparate religions, can find its way to a concordant expression of moral requirements directly related to the realities of today's uncertain world. Likewise, the significance within the realm of business and industry of statements like the Caux Principles and the CERES Principles must not be forgotten. They appear to be more than a mere gesture.

Our world is not dominated by one religious tradition or by one secular credo. This kind of pluralism requires that each and every one of us bring our faith and its insights to the table to share in conversation and deliberation. This is dialogue. In dialogic exchange, all participants retain the integrity of their beliefs but hope that as these beliefs are aired and interpreted in light of common threats a common stance will emerge. The fact that breakthroughs for moral agreement like those just mentioned have actually happened helps to keep us talking.

In dialogue, we witness to our faith while we seek the common good as a testimony to our hope. If Christianity were an ideology that could not take no for an answer and were driven to overpower all who resist it, dialogue would not be possible. But Christianity is secure in its willingness to simply let the Christ stand forth and the Holy Spirit work. We know that our faith in the promise of God in Christ is in the pure grace of that promise; our hope is not in knowing it all, being always right, or staying in control. We are free to engage in the give-and-take of dialogue, to learn from others and modify our views even as we contribute out of a steadfast witness to the deepest insights of our faith. Out of this give-and-take can come the discovery of shared values among people of diverse perspectives and conditions. To keep people talking may be one of the most tangible contributions the church can make to address the world's problems.

## THESIS FOUR: OUR CALL AND OUR ASSURANCE

Our call to address greed and its effects is grounded in assurance rather than certitude.

Many will remember the story of the rich young man recorded in Matthew 19. He came to Jesus asking what he must do to be saved. After an exchange about the Commandments, which the young man assured Jesus he had kept, Jesus tells him that he lacks one thing. If he would be perfect, he should sell all that he has, give it to the poor, and follow Jesus. The man went away "grieving" because he had great wealth.

In *The Cost of Discipleship,* Dietrich Bonhoeffer presents a lengthy reflection on this story.[5] He recognizes that some might say the real issue is faith in Jesus above all. The critical point is not whether or not one has riches. The point is whether they really matter to you, they would argue. One can have wealth and also be a Christian if one can maintain a spirit of inner detachment from those possessions. There is some truth in this apparent sophistry, according to Bonhoeffer. Nevertheless, the "ultimate possibility" this interpretation describes is not the first conclusion we should draw.

Instead, Bonhoeffer writes, we should take Jesus' radical call to obedience at face value. To set it aside too quickly by saying that Jesus didn't mean what he said, that only faith matters, would be to risk cheapening the call to discipleship. Discipleship would, then, be merely a way to claim the comfort of God's forgiveness while finding reasons to do as we please.

On the other hand, to take Jesus' command to the young rich man as a literal statement of what to do to effect our salvation would trivialize the encounter. It would suggest that we had the power to perfectly satisfy God's will, even though it would be a heavy tab for one like the young rich man. Bonhoeffer points out how Jesus' statement in verse 26 deflects us from that path of interpretation. Having just spoken of how difficult it is for the rich to enter "the kingdom of heaven"—this is the camel and the eye of the needle simile—Jesus says that, nonetheless, "with God all things are possible." Salvation is in God's gracious hands.

What, then, has been set before us? Bonhoeffer would say a paradoxical situation or a sustained tension. The call to obey that confronted the rich young man was neither one he could ignore nor one through which he could claim righteousness. Faith does not cancel out obedience, and obedience cannot take the place of faith. "Only he who believes is obedient, and only he who is obedient believes."[6] And both are the work of God's grace.

What does this mean for our own obedience? Most people who read this book will probably have, or at least have the potential for, more wealth than the majority of people in the world. And, most will have an opportunity to participate at some level in the processes for change. So, how do we use what we have, and to what courses of action do we give our support and energy? To repeat an earlier theme, we are in it together. While we can't do it all on our own, there *is* strength in numbers. Even so, as individuals and communities of faith, we are in constant search for the will of God in the decisions we make. We are denied the comfort of a prescribed path of obedience, a set formula. At the same time, we are aware of our capacity to rationalize away the hard choices, covering our half-hearted devotion with sophisticated reasoning.

What does a faithful disciple do? How do we know when we have given enough? What does a faithful church do? How do we know its priorities are the right ones? Is it possible that the church hoards too much of its treasure for its own institutional benefit, a kind of ecclesiastical greed? How can we, as Christians, be certain when we wade into the murky waters of public policy that the things we advocate will really help to stem the tide of greed and fill stomachs and hopes now empty? When systems at work seem to violate the values of sharing, how do we weigh our duty to promote change against the possible threats of reprisal that could endanger our family's income and security? If we choose to act in favor of the latter, have we failed our call? These and countless similar questions lurk in the many crevices of our journey across the terrain of greed. And, the answers will not be framed in certitude. Rather, the answer will be a renewed call to continue our struggle with the questions and to continue to participate.

It is the fact that we are called that sustains us. We are God's people, called to the royal priesthood, called to declare the marvelous deeds of God who has brought us out of darkness into the light (1 Peter 2:8-9). That is our authorization to participate in the struggle, despite its uncertainties. To be called is to be claimed by God's grace. We have no certitude. What we do have is the assurance of God's promised future and of God's promise to be with us on the way to that future.

When the disciples heard this, they were greatly astounded, asking Jesus, "Then who can be saved?" But Jesus looked at them and said, "For mortals it is impossible, but for God all things are possible" (Matthew 19:25-26).

## QUESTIONS FOR DISCUSSION

1. What is your congregation or church body doing to help its members and the church as a whole address the questions raised by the problems associated with greed? What can be done to affirm the vocation of all God's people?
2. Discuss those stewardship programs you are familiar with. What are their strengths and weaknesses in light of this discussion?
3. Are there social ministry organizations affiliated with your church? Do you know of other church-related agencies of this type? How can you support them?
4. As you review what you have learned from this study, what things stand out in your mind and are important to you?

# NOTES

## CHAPTER 1, GREED: A CHARACTER FOR ALL SEASONS

1. M. Hirsch Goldberg, *The Complete Book of Greed* (New York: William Morrow, 1994), 17–32.

2. Ibid., 226–28.

3. Greed, avarice, and covetousness are discussed by James F. Childress under "Covetousness" in *The Westminster Dictionary of Christian Ethics*, ed. James F. Childress and John Macquarrie (Philadelphia: Westminster, 1986), 256.

4. Halvor Moxnes, *The Economy of the Kingdom* (Philadelphia: Fortress Press, 1988), 36–47. Moxnes contrasts this order with a market exchange economy, which is free to follow its own rules because it is not culturally embedded. That contrast is valid, but the cultural embeddedness of convictions about individual freedom and our economy's capacity for unlimited growth that we shall explore in this chapter may not be all that far afield from the ancient patterns in which economic life and cultural expectations and symbols were tightly interwoven.

5. Martin Luther, "The Sermon on the Mount," trans. Jaroslov Pelikan, in *Luther's Works* 21, ed. Jaroslov Pelikan (St. Louis: Concordia, 1956), 12.

6. Martin Luther, "Trade and Usury," *Luther's Works* 45, ed. Walther I. Brandt (Philadelphia: Muhlenberg, 1962), 247.

7. M. Douglas Meeks, *God the Economist* (Minneapolis: Fortress Press, 1989), 37–38.

8. Herman E. Daly and John B. Cobb Jr., *For the Common Good: Redirecting the Economy toward Community, the Environment, and a Sustainable Future*, 2nd ed. (Boston: Beacon, 1994), 89–95.

9. Glenn McGee, *The Perfect Baby* (Lanham, Boulder, New York, London: Rowman and Littlefield, 1997), 31.

10. Comments made during the Hein-Fry Lectures at Trinity Lutheran Seminary, April 15, 1998.

11. Solomon Schimmel, *The Seven Deadly Sins* (New York and Oxford: Oxford University Press, 1997), 173.

12. Hans Küng, "A Global Ethic in an Age of Globalization," *Business Ethics Quarterly*, vol. 7, no. 3 (July 1997), 23.

13. Graef S. Crystal, *In Search of Excess* (New York and London: Norton, 1991), 27–28.

14. Harrison Rainie, with Margaret Loftus and Mark Madden, "The State of Greed" in *U.S. News and World Report* (June 17, 1996), 68.

15. Robert N. Bellah, Richard Madsen, William M. Sullivan, Ann Swidler, and Steven Tipton, *Habits of the Heart: Individualism and Commitment in American Life* (Berkeley: University of California Press, 1985), 296.
16. Michael Novak, "Habits of the Left-Wing Heart," *National Review* 37 (June 28, 1985), 36.
17. Benjamin Barber, Review, *New Republic* 192 (May 20, 1985), 33.
18. Nicholas A. Christakis, "Managing Death: The Growing Acceptance of Euthanasia in Contemporary Culture," *Must We Suffer Our Way to Death?* ed. Ronald P. Hamel and Edwin R. DuBose (Dallas: Southern Methodist University Press, 1996), 15–38.
19. Barber, 36.
20. Laurence Shames, *The Hunger for More: Searching for Values in an Age of Greed* (New York: Vintage, 1991), 21–22.
21. Ibid., 23.
22. James Eggert, *What Is Economics?* 3rd ed. (Mountain View, Calif.: Mayfield, 1993), 104–7.
23. Larry L. Rasmussen, *Earth Community, Earth Ethics* (Maryknoll, N.Y.: Orbis, 1996), 112–13.
24. Ibid., 168–69.
25. Stuart L. Hart, "Beyond Greening: Strategies for a Sustainable World," *Harvard Business Review* (January/February 1997), 66–76, and Joan Magretta, "Growth through Global Sustainability: An Interview with Monsanto's CEO, Robert B. Shapiro," 79–88.
26. I am indebted to my colleague Ralph W. Doermann for his helpful and durable pamphlet, "Biblical Concern for the Poor," written for the Commission on Church and Society of the American Lutheran Church, 1972.
27. L. T. Hobhouse, *Liberalism* (London: Oxford University Press, 1964), 50–51, offers one example. Hobhouse published this work in 1911.

### CHAPTER 2, FROM PARABLE TO PARADIGM

1. John Dominic Crossan, *In Parables: The Challenge of the Historical Jesus* (New York: Harper and Row, 1973), 67–68; Walter Pilgrim, *Good News to the Poor: Wealth and Poverty in Luke-Acts* (Minneapolis: Augsburg, 1981), 113–19; Richard J. Bauckham, "The Rich Man and Lazarus: The Parable and the Parallels," *New Testament Studies* 37 (April 1991), 245.
2. Crossan, *In Parables*, 67; Pilgrim, *Good News to the Poor*, 116; Bauckham, "The Rich Man and Lazarus," 231–37.
3. Pilgrim, *Good News to the Poor*, 106.
4. Moxnes, *The Economy of the Kingdom* (Philadelphia: Fortress Press, 1988), 76ff.
5. Ibid., 73, 83.
6. Ibid., 88–89.
7. Martin Luther, "Trade and Usury," *Luther's Works* 45, ed. Walther I. Brandt (Philadelphia: Muhlenberg, 1962), 248.
8. Moxnes, *The Economy of the Kingdom*, 94–96.
9. Pilgrim, *Good News to the Poor*, 149–51.

10. Moxnes, *Economy of the Kingdom,* 146–57. See also Walter Taylor, "Obligation: Paul's Foundation for Ethics," *Trinity Seminary Review,* 19.2 (Fall/Winter 1997), 91–112.

11. Moxnes, *Economy of the Kingdom,* 112.

12. Ibid., 152.

13. Marc J. Cohen, "World Hunger in a Global Economy," *Hunger in a Global Economy* (Silver Spring, Md.: Bread for the World Institute, 1998), 21.

14. Gerhard von Rad, *Old Testament Theology,* vol. 1, trans. D. M. G. Stalker (New York: Harper and Row, 1962), 141–44.

15. Walther Eichrodt, *Theology of the Old Testament,* vol. 2, trans. J. A. Baker (Philadelphia: Westminster, 1967), 126–27.

16. C. F. D. Moule, in *Man and Nature in the New Testament,* Facet Books Biblical Series 17 (Philadelphia: Fortress Press, 1967), 2–4, made this point, which has been reiterated countless times since in the context of the debate over whether or not this passage from Genesis has been the basis of Judeo-Christian neglect for environmentalism.

17. Gerhard von Rad, *Genesis,* trans. John H. Marks (Philadelphia: Westminster, 1961), 57–58.

18. Robert Frost, "There Are Roughly Limits," *The Poetry of Robert Frost,* ed. Edward Connery Lathem (New York: Holt, Rinehart, and Winston, 1969), 305.

19. Dietrich Bonhoeffer, *Creation and Fall, Temptation* (New York: Macmillan, 1959), 37.

20. I have dealt in detail with the doctrine of the image of God and the New Testament development of the doctrine in *Christian Anthropology and Ethics* (Philadelphia: Fortress Press, 1978), see especially 98–99, 117–18.

21. Karl Barth, *Church Dogmatics,* vol. 3, trans. G. T. Thompson (New York: Charles Scribner's Sons, 1936), 183ff., 195ff.

22. This idea is brought out powerfully in one of Karl Barth's early lectures. See *Ethics,* ed. Dietrich Braun, trans. Geoffrey W. Bromily (New York: Seabury, 1981), 456.

23. See the discussion of this point in Joseph Sittler, *The Structure of Christian Ethics* (Baton Rouge: Louisiana State University Press, 1958), 36–38.

24. Michael Ball, "The Parables of the Unjust Steward and the Rich Man and Lazarus," *Expository Times* 106 (August 1995), 329–30.

## CHAPTER 3, THE BUSINESS OF BUSINESS IS AVARICE?

1. Marjorie Kelly, "Why 'Socially Responsible' Isn't Enough," *Business Ethics,* vol. 11, no. 4 (July/August 1997), 5.

2. I have made my own contribution to this discussion in James M. Childs Jr., "Lutheran Perspectives on Ethical Business in an Age of Downsizing," *Business Ethics Quarterly,* vol. 7, no. 2 (March 1997), 123–31. Some of the observations in this section of the chapter derive from work done on that article.

3. Louis Uchitelle and N. R. Kleinfield, "One of the Battlefields of Business, Millions of Casualties," "The Downsizing of America," *New York Times,*

March 3, 1996, 1ff. See also my discussion of this material in Childs, "Lutheran Perspectives on Ethical Business."

4. Ibid., 2.

5. Aaron Bernstein, "This Job Market Still Has Plenty of Slack," *Business Week* (June 24, 1996), 36.

6. "The State of Greed," *U.S. News and World Report* (June 14, 1996), 63.

7. Russell Baker, "Economy's Victims Want No Sermons," *Columbus Dispatch* (March 26, 1996), 7A.

8. Alan Downs, *Corporate Executions: The Ugly Truth about Layoffs—How Corporate Greed Is Shattering Lives, Companies, and Communities* (New York: American Management Association, 1995).

9. Claudia H. Deutsch, "Kodak Plans More Job Cuts But Posts Profit for Quarter," *New York Times on the Web* (July 22, 1999).

10. Frederick Maidment and William Eldridge, *Business in Government and Society: Ethical, International Decision Making* (Upper Saddle River, N.J.: Prentice Hall, 2000), 8.

11. For an example, see the comments on former CEO of AT&T Robert Allen in John Dalla Costa, *The Ethical Imperative: Why Moral Leadership Is Good Business* (Reading, Mass.: Addison-Wesley, 1998), 274.

12. Graef S. Crystal, *In Search of Excess: The Overcompensation of American Executives* (New York and London: Norton, 1991), 24–26.

13. See, for example, Jerry Mander and John Cavanaugh, "WTO Feeds Corporate Greed," *USA Today* (December 2, 1999), 14A.

14. Crystal, *In Search of Excess*, 27–28.

15. Ibid., 99–109.

16. *Business Week* (April 1997), 59–62, cited in Dalla Costa, *The Ethical Imperative*, 56.

17. Timothy L. O'Brien, "Handsome Pay for the Co-Chairman of Citigroup," *New York Times on the Web* (March 19, 1999).

18. Michael Novak, *Business as a Calling: Work and the Examined Life* (New York: The Free Press, 1996), 11.

19. "Seeing Things as They Really Are," *Forbes* (March 1997), 124, quoted in Dalla Costa, *The Ethical Imperative*, 48.

20. Heidi Vernon, *Business and Society: A Managerial Approach*, 6th ed. (New York: McGraw-Hill, 1998), 7.

21. Richard B. Freeman, "Toward an Apartheid Economy?" *Harvard Business Review*, vol. 74, no. 5 (September/October 1996), 114.

22. Ibid., 120. In a more recent article Frank Levy, Professor of Urban Economics at M.I.T, reviewed two books that took opposite views on the income gap. Levy ends up recognizing that both the optimistic and the pessimistic versions of the income gap debate have merit, but, in the final analysis a high degree of inequality in our society is real and dangerous if left unaddressed. Frank Levy, "Rhetoric and Reality: Making Sense of the Income Gap Debate," *Harvard Business Review* (September/October 1999), 163–70.

23. Martin Luther, "Trade and Usury," *Luther's Works* 45, ed. Walther I. Brandt (Philadelphia: Muhlenberg, 1962), 251.

24. Karl Holl, *The Cultural Significance of the Reformation*, trans. Karl Hertz, Barbara Hertz, and John H. Lichtbblau (New York: World, 1959), 77.

25. Carter Lindberg, *Beyond Charity: Reformation Initiatives for the Poor* (Minneapolis: Fortress Press, 1993), 100–104.

26. The principal locations for Luther's "two kingdoms" doctrine are "Temporal Authority: To What Extent It Should Be Obeyed," *Luther's Works*, vol. 45, ed. Walther I. Brandt (Philadelphia: Muhlenberg, 1962), 75– 129, and "The Sermon on the Mount," *Luther's Works*, vol. 21, ed. Jaroslav Pelikan (St. Louis: Concordia, 1956), 1–294.

27. Luther's writings are replete with references to reform of society as well as church. To cite just one example, see "To the Christian Nobility of the German Nation Concerning the Reform of the Christian Estate," *Luther's Works* 44, ed. Helmut T. Lehmann (Philadelphia: Fortress Press, 1966), 115–217.

28. I have written a brief history of this development of Luther's thought; see James M. Childs Jr., "Ethics and the Promise of God: Moral Authority and the Church's Witness," in *The Promise of Lutheran Ethics*, ed. Karen L. Bloomquist and John R. Stumme (Minneapolis: Fortress Press, 1998), 97–114.

29. For a good historical analysis of the Lutheran two realms tradition, see Karl Hertz, *Two Kingdoms and One World* (Minneapolis: Augsburg, 1976).

30. James M. Childs Jr., *Ethics in Business: Faith at Work* (Minneapolis: Fortress Press, 1995), 21–26.

31. Downs, *Corporate Executions*, 164.

32. Ibid., 164–67.

33. Michael A. B. Boddington, Alan Own, and Robin Heal, "British Petroleum and Economic Redevelopment in South Wales," Council for Ethics in Economics (Columbus, Ohio: November 1995).

34. "The State of Greed," 63–64.

## CHAPTER 4, UNSHARED GOODS: HEALTH CARE IN AMERICA

1. Wendell Berry, *What Are People For?* (San Francisco: North Point, 1990), 85.

2. Ibid., 85–86.

3. Ellyn E. Spragins, "Does Managed Care Work?" *Newsweek* (September 28, 1998), 60.

4. Ibid.

5. James Nelson, *Human Medicine: Ethical Perspectives on New Medical Issues* (Minneapolis: Augsburg, 1973), 174–75.

6. Ibid.

7. *Ethical Considerations in the Business Aspects of Health Care*, Woodstock Theological Center (Washington, D.C.: Georgetown University Press, 1995), 4.

8. Christine Cassell, "The Patient-Physician Covenant: An Affirmation of Asklepios," *Annals of Internal Medicine*, vol. 13, no. 18 (July 19, 1996), 31.

9. "Patient-Physician Covenant," *Journal of the American Medical Association* (May 17, 1995).

10. *Journal of the American Medical Association* (December 3, 1997).

11. Robert Reno, "Fibbing Is Just What the Doctor Ordered," *Columbus Dispatch* (November 18, 1998), 11A.

12. Julie A. Jacob, "HMO Top Salaries Average $2 Million in 1997," *American Medical News* (October 5, 1998), 24.

13. See Chris Rauber, "HMO Exodus Continues," *Modern Healthcare*, vol. 28, no. 4 (October 5, 1998), 3; Chris Rauber, "Exit with Caution: FLA Investigates HMOs Leaving Medicare Markets," *Modern Healthcare*, vol. 28, no 6 (October 19, 1998), 2; and Spragnis, "Does Managed Care Work?" 63.

14. *Ethical Considerations in the Business Aspects of Health Care*, Woodstock, 16–18.

15. Milt Freudenheim, "Big H.M.O. to Give Decisions on Care Back to Doctors," *New York Times on the Web* (November 9, 1999), New York Times Archive Article.

16. Daniel Callahan, *Setting Limits: Medical Goals in an Aging Society* (New York: Simon and Schuster, 1987), passim.

17. Daniel Callahan, *False Hopes: Why America's Quest for Perfect Health Is a Recipe for Failure* (New York: Simon and Schuster, 1998).

18. Harmon L. Smith, *Ethics and the New Medicine* (Nashville and New York: Abingdon, 1970), 125.

19. Martin Luther, *A Treatise on Christian Liberty*, trans. W. A. Lambert, rev. Harold J. Grimm (Philadelphia: Fortress Press, 1957), 30.

20. Wolfhart Pannenberg, *What Is Man?* trans. Duane A. Priebe (Philadelphia: Fortress Press, 1970), 28–40.

21. Philip S. Keane, *Health Care Reform: A Catholic View* (New York: Paulist, 1993), 185.

22. Callahan, *False Hopes*, 113.

### CHAPTER 5, UNSHARED GOODS: HUNGER AND THE GLOBAL ECONOMY

1. See Richard de George, *Business Ethics*, 3rd ed. (New York: Macmillan, 1990), 3–5.

2. *Christian Faith and the World Economy Today* (Geneva: World Council of Churches, 1992), 4–5.

3. John Dalla Costa, *The Ethical Imperative: Why Moral Leadership Is Good Business* (Reading, Mass.: Addison-Wesley, 1998), 20–28.

4. Ibid., 135–37.

5. Reprinted in part in Hans Küng, "A Global Ethic in an Age of Globalization," *Business Ethics Quarterly*, vol. 7, no. 3 (July 1997), 29–30.

6. *Hunger in a Global Economy*, Eighth Annual Report on the State of World Hunger (Silver Spring, Md.: Bread for the World Institute, 1998).

7. Daniel Finn, *Just Trading: On the Ethics and Economics of International Trade* (Nashville: Abingdon Press, 1996), 136–46.

8. *Hunger in a Global Economy*, 48.

9. Patrick McMahon, "Trade Talks Open; Groups Vow More Protests Today," *USA Today* (December 2, 1999), 1–2A.

10. Barend A. De Vries, *Champions of the Poor: The Economic Consequences of Judeo-Christian Values* (Washington, D.C.: Georgetown University Press, 1998), 230–53.

## CHAPTER 6, TOWARD A SHARING SOCIETY

1. Henri Nouwen, "Bearing Fruit in the Spirit," *Sojourners,* vol. 14, no. 7 (July 1985), 30.

2. The account of the Davos forum is gleaned from Associated Press news releases, January 30, 1999, and January 31, 1999, published by America Online, and James Flanigan's syndicated report "World's Best, Brightest Meet to Improve Global Economy," *Columbus Dispatch* (January 31, 1999), 3F.

3. John Dalla Costa, *The Ethical Imperative: Why Moral Leadership Is Good Business* (Reading, Mass.: Addison-Wesley, 1998), 87–88.

4. Ibid., 104.

5. Herman Daly, *Beyond Growth: The Economics of Sustainable Development* (Boston: Beacon, 1996).

6. Mark Sagoff, "Do We Consume Too Much?" SIRS Researcher, World Wide Web, 1–3.

7. See Herman Daly, "Reply to Mark Sagoff's 'Carrying Capacity and Ecological Economics,'" in *Ethics of Consumption: The Good Life, Justice, and Global Stewardship,* ed. David A. Crocker and Toby Linden (Lanham, Md.: Rowman and Littlefield, 1998), 53–62.

8. Herman E. Daly and John B. Cobb Jr., *For the Common Good: Redirecting the Economy toward Community, the Environment, and a Sustainable Future,* 2nd ed. (Boston: Beacon, 1994), 8–15.

9. Michael Novak, *Free Persons and the Common Good* (New York: Madison, 1989), 88–89.

10. Ibid., 83.

11. *Christian Faith and the World Economy Today* (Geneva: World Council of Churches, 1992), 37.

12. Wolfhart Pannenberg, *Theology and the Kingdom of God* (Philadelphia: Westminster, 1969), 126.

13. *Christian Faith and the World Economy Today,* 41, cites a study of debt relief by Harvard economist Jeffrey Sachs, published in *The Economist* (October 12, 1991).

## CHAPTER 7, STAKEHOLDER CAPITALISM: A CASE STUDY IN SHARING

1. Adam Smith, *An Inquiry into the Nature and Cause of the Wealth of Nations,* ed. R. H. Campbell, A. S. Skinner, and W. B. Todd (Oxford: Clarendon Press, 1976), IV, ii, 9.

2. Jon M. Shepard, James C. Wimbush, and Carroll U. Stephens, "The Place of Ethics in Business: Shifting Paradigms?" *Business Ethics Quarterly,* vol. 5, no. 3 (1995), 592.

3. Ibid.

4. James Q. Wilson, "Adam Smith on Business Ethics," *California Management Review* (fall 1989), 59–64.

5. Shepard, et. al, "The Place of Ethics in Business," 594–96.

6. Ibid., 595. See also Robert C. Solomon, *The New World of Business: Ethics and Free Enterprise in the Global 1990s* (Lanham, Md.: Rowman and Littlefield, 1993), 203–86, a section entitled "Social Responsibility: Society and Stakeholder."

7. J. Richard Finlay, "Ethics and Accountability: The Rising Power of Stakeholder Capitalism," *On Moral Business*, ed. Max L. Stackhouse, Dennis P. McCann, Shirley J. Roels, and Preston N. Williams (Grand Rapids: Eerdmans, 1995), 898.

8. Richard de George, *Business Ethics*, 3rd ed. (New York: Macmillan, 1990), 163–64.

9. Heidi Vernon, *Business and Society: A Managerial Approach*, 6th ed. (New York: McGraw-Hill, 1998), 88.

10. Ibid., 89. Vernon is citing the work of Jeffrey S. Harrison and Caron H. St. John in the *Academy of Management Executive*, vol. 10, no. 2 (1966), 46–60.

11. R. Edward Freeman and Jeanne Liedka, "Corporate Social Responsibility: A Critical Approach," *Business Horizons* (July/August 1991), 92–98, as cited in Vernon, *Business and Society*, 27–28.

12. Laura Nash, *Good Intentions Aside: A Manager's Guide to Resolving Ethical Problems* (Boston: Harvard Business School Press, 1990), 95.

13. R. Edward Freeman, "Poverty and the Politics of Capitalism," *Business Ethics Quarterly: The Ruffin Series*, no. 1 (1998), 32.

14. Robert A. Phillips, "Stakeholder Theory and a Principle of Fairness," *Business Ethics Quarterly*, vol. 7, no. 1 (January 1997), 63.

15. Ibid., 64.

16. Margaret M. Blair, *Ownership and Control: Rethinking Corporate Governance for the Twenty-First Century* (Washington, D.C.: The Brookings Institution, 1995), 5, 223–25.

17. See the discussion of this point in a colloquium on Margaret Blair's work: Blair, *Wealth Creation and Wealth Sharing* (Washington, D.C.: The Brookings Institution, 1996), 12.

18. Blair, *Ownership and Control*, 224–25.

19. Ibid., 239–74.

20. Ibid., 238, 329; Blair, *Wealth Creation and Wealth Sharing*, 8.

21. Blair, *Ownership and Control*, 239–40, and passim.

22. Blair, *Wealth Creation and Wealth Sharing*, 3.

23. Lynn Sharp Paine, "Managing for Organizational Integrity," *Harvard Business Review* (March/April 1994), 106–17.

## CHAPTER 8, TEACH YOUR CHILDREN WELL

1. Juliet B. Schor, *The Overspent American: Upscaling, Downshifting, and the New Consumer* (New York: Basic Books, 1998), 93–94.

2. Ibid., 21.

3. *Affluenza*, a coproduction of KCTS/Seattle and Oregon Public Broadcasting (Bullfrog Films, 1997).

4. Cornel West, *Race Matters* (Boston: Beacon Press, 1993), 16–17.

5. Schor, *The Overspent American*, 54–57.

6. Ibid., 85–88.

7. Ibid.

8. James M. Childs Jr., *Faith, Formation, and Decision: Ethics in the Community of Promise* (Minneapolis: Fortress Press, 1992), 29–30.

9. James A. Nash, "Toward the Revival and Reform of the Subversive Virtue: Frugality," *Annual of the Society for Christian Ethics 1995*, ed. Harlan Beckley (Boston: Society for Christian Ethics, 1995), 135–60.

10. Ibid., 154.

11. Larry L. Rasmussen, *Moral Fragments and Moral Community* (Minneapolis: Fortress Press, 1993), 106.

12. Wendell Berry, *Another Turn of the Crank: Essays* (Washington, D.C. : Counterpoint, 1995), 5–7.

13. John F. Freie, *Counterfeit Community: The Exploitation of Our Longings for Connectedness* (Lanham, Boulder, New York, and Oxford: Rowman and Littlefield, 1998), passim.

14. Stewart W. Herman, *Durable Goods: A Covenantal Ethic for Management and Employees* (Notre Dame: University of Notre Dame Press, 1997), 191–92.

15. Suzy Wetlaufer, "Driving Change: An Interview with Ford Motor Company's Jacques Nasser," *Harvard Business Review* (March/April 1999), 87.

## CHAPTER 9, A QUESTION OF CALLING

1. *Greed with John Stossel*, ABC News Special, March 11, 1999.

2. Laura Nash, *Good Intentions Aside: A Manager's Guide to Resolving Ethical Problems* (Boston: Harvard Business School Press, 1990), 51–79.

3. Quoted in James A. Nash, "Toward the Revival and Reform of the Subversive Virtue: Frugality," *Annual of the Society for Christian Ethics 1995*, ed. Harlan Beckley (Boston: Society for Christian Ethics, 1995), 154.

4. Harvey Cox, "The Market as God," *Atlantic Monthly*, vol. 283, no. 3 (March 1999), 23.

5. Dietrich Bonhoeffer, *The Cost of Discipleship* (New York: Macmillan, 1963), 77–94.

6. Ibid., 69.

# INDEX